Building From The Top, And Other Readings

BUILDING FROM THE TOP;

AND

OTHER READINGS.

BUILDING FROM THE TOP;

AND

OTHER READINGS.

BUILDING FROM THE TOP;

AND

OTHER READINGS.

BY THE

REV. WILLIAM HASLAM, M.A.,

*Formerly Rector of Buckenham, Norwich, and late Incumbent
of Curzon Chapel, Mayfair;
Author of " The Threefold Gift of God," " Personal
Experience," &c.*

London:
JARROLD & SONS, 3, PATERNOSTER BUILDINGS.

PREFACE.

HE narratives which form this volume have already had a very large circulation in separate tracts. Having reason to know that they have been blessed to many souls, the Author has been encouraged to issue them again in their present form, with attractive illustrations, in the hope that, under the Divine blessing, their usefulness may be greatly increased and extended.

The reader will observe that the stories, one after another, set forth the absolute necessity of that spiritual change which is called in Holy Scripture the New Birth. In one form or another this vital subject is dwelt upon and enforced, both with encouragements and warnings. Here also may be seen not only the spiritual change wrought, but also the manner in which souls were awakened, and how they were dealt with.

May believers, in reading this book, be encouraged to win souls; and those who are not yet believers be directed to seek salvation, and never rest till they know the peace of God which passeth all understanding.

CONTENTS.

	PAGE
BUILDING FROM THE TOP	11
OLD BILLY; OR, SPARED TO BE SAVED	19
THE FAMILY OF FOUR	27
FORGIVENESS; OR, THE USEFUL MISTAKE	36
NINES AND SIXES	43
THE ELECT; OR, VIEWS OF HIS OWN	50
THE BETHEL FLAG	59
WHAT A SHAME	66
THE SILVER LADDER	75
RICHARD'S VICTORY	82
NOT A WALL, BUT A DOOR	91
THE LORD'S MESSENGER	98
THE "SECOND LOOK"	107
THE MOTHER'S PRAYER	114
THE GOOD OLD GENTLEMAN	123
OVER THE RIVER	129
POOR EVA	139
MARY; THE CHILD OF GOD	146
TRUE OR FALSE PEACE	155

10 CONTENTS.

		PAGE
THE PILOT'S FLAG		162
GOING HOME OR LEAVING HOME?		171
THE KEY OF HEAVEN		177
THE DOCTOR'S STORY		187
THE DYING GIPSY		193

BUILDING FROM THE TOP.

—◆—

ILL YOU BEGIN TO BUILD YOUR SPIRE FROM THE TOP?" said an elderly Christian lady, who was sitting in her wheel-chair, and had been calmly listening to the conversation which was passing in the room. Her question was gravely addressed to an ardent young clergyman, who was at that time very busy in a new District to which he had recently been appointed.

He was full of his plans, and was telling of his temporary Church and Schools, and Parochial Clubs, and the *new Church* which he was building. A nobleman in the neighbourhood had ordered the tower of it to be raised higher, and a spire to surmount it; and another noble person had ordered a peal of six bells for this new tower.

Our young friend's heart was very full of thankfulness and hope, and out of the abundance of his gladness he went on to say what services there were to be in the new Church, and to speak about the organ and the choir, the painted window, and how he was now gathering his congregation.

The lady had been silently listening to all this, and when there was a little pause, asked her question,—

"WILL YOU BEGIN TO BUILD YOUR SPIRE FROM THE TOP?"

"Oh, grandmamma!" said several voices at once; but the lady *meant* something, and looked for an answer; and this was complacently given. "No, not from the top, but from the foundation."

The lady said, "That is right—that is right," and went on with her knitting. But the question was a strange one, nor was it spoken in jest or in ignorance. It was like a riddle, but what did it mean?

The subject of conversation was changed, yet the person to whom the question was addressed could not forget it, or the significant look with which it was asked.

Soon after this the lady was taken away, but the words remained and were associated in the clergyman's mind and memory with their author. Time passed on, the Church tower, with its spire, was completed and consecrated with great ceremony and joyfulness. The intended services were duly commenced and continued, and everything was as successful as the heart of the clergyman could desire; there was no drawback. It was a beautiful Church, the admiration of the neighbourhood, and quite a striking object, situated as it was in a wild and elevated part of a large populous parish.

The people were content with dry, dead, empty husks and formal ceremonies! for though the services were reverently performed, and were very orderly, hearty, animating, cheerful, and attractive, and the sermon sensible, earnest, and useful; yet alas! *spiritual death reigned there* in the midst. The Lord was not there; what is more, the Holy Spirit was not sought, therefore did not breathe on the slain; and what was worse than all, there was no sense or suspicion of need!

About this time a tract, called "The Great Error Detected,"* was given to our earnest friend, marked in several places with pencil, to attract his attention. He read there of JOHN BERRIDGE, with some interest; for his first history in some measure corresponded with his own.

* Published by the Religious Tract Society. No. 280.

As he went on reading he wondered, Can this be *building from the top*, to begin with sanctification before justification? But what did Berridge mean by justification? What was that "wondrous thing which God did, for his soul and the souls of his people?" What could he mean by having "his eyes opened to see himself a wretched lost man, and seeing the way of salvation?" Berridge said he had "preached for six years and never brought a soul to Christ;" and for two years more in another parish, and had no success; but now, when he preached CHRIST, the people came from all parts, far and near, to hear the glorious sound of the Gospel. Some came six miles, some eight, and some ten, and that constantly; and "believers were added to the church continually." What was all this?

Ah, reader, perhaps you little think how ignorant people are who do not know! All these things, however, set our friend pondering and wondering; but he could not solve the difficulty, for words and definitions, and descriptions of experience on spiritual matters only raised greater perplexities which they could not answer, for spiritual things can only be spiritually discerned. Yet, notwithstanding, he endeavoured to grapple with the subject, though he could not by searching find out anything! He was in the dark, and knew not yet that he himself was blind and ignorant, and needed the power of the Holy Spirit to awaken him, and bring him to see himself as he was—a lost sinner, and to make him feel his need of a Saviour to pardon and deliver him.

Time passed on, and with it manifold works, and many services—forms of godliness without the power thereof, till it pleased God to bring him to a faithful friend, who said to him abruptly one day, "*You will never do any good in your parish till you are converted*," for he was actually building up people before he had brought them in. He was indignant and contemptuous, and thought this loving and true word was very personal (so it was) and very abusive. In fact, the strong man armed, within, who had been keeping his goods in *peace*, was assailed by these words, and there was a brief tempest of anger; but the calmness and assurance of the person who spoke them was undoubting, and there was no appearance of mistake or misgiving. Subsequent conversation, instead of acquitting him, only brought up another fundamental point on which he was deficient.

"You don't know," said his true kind friend, "*the difference between the natural conscience and the work of the Holy Spirit.*"

He was honestly at a loss now, yet still somehow he endeavoured to battle it out. The next day reading the Word, he came to this passage, which quite arrested him: "Depart from me, all ye workers of iniquity" (Luke xiii. 27); and the question arose in his mind, "What if he says this to me? but He will not say it to me." Nevertheless the question haunted him,—"What if He does?"

Evidently shrinking away from the searching word, he thought of all his righteousness,—how he had openly renounced the world and its pleasures, and he remembered his devotion, zeal, religiousness, daily service, and strict attention to parochial visitations and schools. He recalled to his mind his conscious and intentional efforts for the glory of God; all this was pleaded in thought; but the reader will observe it was evasion and self-justification, and this was his only plea!

Being alone now, he began to tremble at his own thoughts; and he went on to read the passage more carefully. Then another thought met him, it was this: that all those to whom the Lord spoke were *taken by surprise;* they had evidently been building from the top without any foundation, therefore were rejected when they looked for welcome! and they cried out in their amazement, "Lord, Lord, we have eaten and drunk in Thy presence, and Thou hast taught in our streets." And in another Gospel, such as these are made to say—"Lord, Lord, we have prophesied in Thy name, and in Thy name have cast out devils, and in Thy name done many wonderful works?" But nevertheless He professed to them, "I never knew you: depart from me, ye that work iniquity!" (Matt. vii. 22, 23.)

Our friend's soul was more and more agitated, for he could not say he had prophesied, or cast out devils, or done any wonderful works, and if persons gifted with such great talents were liable to final rejection, what hope could there be for him? The circle was narrowing and the bands becoming closer, and so he tried to leap out of the net by thinking,—"If I am as bad as all this, I have misled other people, which is not likely." But this device failed also, and fell back on himself with more crushing power.

Was he indeed wrong, and had he been wrong all along, and had he deceived and misled others, many of whom were now beyond his reach, and gone to their awful account? Saul of Tarsus slew the bodies of happy Christians and released their souls to heaven; but he had been slaying *souls!* This was indeed an overwhelming conviction, and it filled his soul with darkness and despair, for he saw that he was guilty of blood—the blood of souls! There, in the churchyard of that beautiful church with the lofty spire, lay the bodies of several good earnest church-men whom he had jealously guarded from intrusion of "Gospel-men," and whom he had zealously and carefully taught, or rather mis-taught. Alas! they were gone without reconciliation and peace, and "there is no repentance or forgiveness in the grave!" How restless and wretched was he now, poor man; and how dark was the misery in which he was engulphed!

On the following Sunday morning he was unwell, and unfit in mind and body to minister at the public service. It was a bright cheerful morning in October, and the bells struck out earlier than usual a merry peal, which sounded away to a great distance, and many people were responding to their musical call, so he roused himself up and went to Church. The service was very soothing, the

Psalms and portions of ·Scripture seemed especially to speak to *him;* the hymns greatly comforted him, and he went up into the pulpit briefly to explain the gospel of the morning, purposing then to return home. He took for his text: "WHAT THINK YE OF CHRIST?" (Matt. xxii. 42,) and as he pursued his discourse, he saw how Jesus, the Son of God, came to save and deliver sinners from the power of sin and the devil, but that the Pharisees were so taken up with themselves, their ritual, services, and atoning sacrifices, that they could not see Christ as He was, though He was there speaking to them, and appealing to His miracles and to the word for testimony of His divinity. Besides, they were looking for a *future* deliverer, and overlooking a *present* One!

While he was thus enabled to speak, and plainly to see the mistake of the Pharisees, he could not but see and feel he had been making exactly the *same mistake himself*— therefore, against him also were launched those awful words of the twenty-third chapter of St. Matthew: "Ye serpents, ye generation of vipers, how shall ye escape the damnation of hell!" "Ye whited sepulchres!"

These Pharisees and Scribes were not careless and immoral or prayerless men: no, far from it. They were religious to a degree, and yet these awful denunciations! Why? because they overlooked Christ as the *Son of Abraham*, now come to be offered, and looked for the Son of David, to restore them to glory! and, in fact, they had overlooked the necessity of a change of heart, and forgiveness of sins through the Blood of the Lamb. But in the midst of the discourse, it pleased the Lord to shew to our friend that *Christ* was the *true and only foundation*, and—what the Pharisee did not see—that He was the Lamb of God who beareth away the sin of the world! Now he saw that to work *for* life was building without a foundation, and promoting sanctification before justification; it was really beginning at the top; building, in imagination, in the air.

Our friend, once laid on the true Foundation, continued the labours of his office with heart set free, and zeal increased; how free, only those can tell who have themselves tasted release from the bondage of unbelief and spiritual death, to the liberty of a joyful loving life; how zealous, those can tell who have felt the power of love within—welling up as from a fountain, and flowing down a living and life-giving stream of glory to God, and service of good-will to men. Now he preached Christ Jesus the Lord, as the Saviour to sinners, and not, as heretofore, doctrines to be believed and ordinances to be obeyed, in the hope of getting salvation at some future time! Not that doctrines and ordinances were to be neglected, far from it, but now they were placed in their proper position, namely, doctrines to *saved sinners*, as means through which their spiritual life was to be nourished; and ordinances, blessed channels through which grateful adoring love might flow up towards God, in obedience to His will. Doctrines and ordinances are as the robe and throne of the King, not the King himself, whose prerogative alone it is to pardon and deliver the guilty.

Now that Christ was lifted up, multitudes of people were brought from many parts to hear the Word of Life, and he who in former time, was so weak in body that he could scarcely get on with such services as he had, was now enabled to do more, and preach every evening besides, and thrice on Sunday, to a church full of anxious and attentive hearers! He who before was satisfied if he succeeded in delivering his sermon creditably, was now not content, though the large congregation was moved to tears under the word of God; he longed for and expected to hear the question of the anxious soul, "What must I do to be saved?"

It became necessary to establish an after service, or meeting in the adjoining school-room, where prayer was made for souls impressed under the Word, and where opportunity was afforded to such to plead for themselves, and they were instructed by experienced persons to look to Christ, and to venture on the Blood which has been shed for sin, thanking God for His mercy.

B

Many, as John Berridge said, were added to the Church who will have occasion to praise God to all eternity. There was a great outpouring of the Holy Spirit on that neighbourhood, and on the congregation of that same church, with the Tower and Spire. *Now* the edification was "from the foundation," and not from the top; now the Christian lady's words were remembered with respect, and the question which sounded so foolish was found to be really a solemn and serious one.

There is one thing more should be said concerning our changed friend; *he* was not ashamed or afraid to declare openly that he had been wrong before, that he had been unconsciously and unintentionally it is true, but still cruelly and fatally misleading souls! Many of his people, seeing his former earnestness and devotion, had thought he was converted, and he might have availed himself of this to pass himself off as one that had always been right; but before God he dared not, and desired it not: therefore, he plainly affirmed, "If I had died last week, I should have been lost for ever!" How could he otherwise have glorified God for His unspeakable mercy? We lose two great points of power and influence when we shrink from confessing our past faults and short-comings, or fear to make open and thankful acknowledgment of our deliverance. Professions as to one's present state and intentions are never so effectual as first the confession and then the burst of thanksgiving! He that covereth his sins can never prosper, whether he be the unpardoned conscious sinner who is justifying himself, or the pardoned and justified sinner who is endeavouring to imply that he never was a sinner.

Reader, be built upon *the* Foundation, the tried, precious corner-stone, CHRIST JESUS; and build on that foundation yourself, not "wood, hay, stubble," but "gold, silver, and precious stones" (1 Cor. iii. 11—15). Worse than building on sand is the foolishness of beginning to "build from the top."

OLD BILLY; OR, SPARED TO BE SAVED.

HOARY head is a crown of glory when it is found in the way of righteousness, but pitiable is it when men and women far advanced in years are in the way of sin and still pressing on to endless ruin! The fires of their youth are quenched, the energy of life departed, their capacity for worldly enjoyments has ceased, and yet they cannot stop, they seem to drift like a doomed ship to the lee shore!

Old Billy was one of these, and moreover like one who was determined to go on, in spite of every remonstrance. He was not without some knowledge of good things either, and he was surrounded by friends and relations who were walking in the ways of God, but he seemed as if he would shew how reckless and daring he could be. It is a hard battle that such people have to fight, and they cannot always do it, or persevere in doing it, without resorting to swearing and other such vehemence to assist them in their course, and to drive off their true friends; or to intoxicating drink, to drown their conscience and exhilarate themselves in spite of it, with a false and transient mirth.

Poor old Billy, he was one of these, and he lived apparently a reckless life, and used to curse and swear as if he really meant evil and wicked ill-will to those against whom he launched his awful oaths; and then again he was continually seen reeling about in drunkenness, singing portions of hymns; or he would stop and talk anxiously about religion.

People used to call old Billy the "lost soul;" the very children in the lanes called after him, "Ah, Billy, you are a lost soul," and laughed at him; and in his rage he swore at them, and said he would murder them and such like.

I could not help regarding this pitiable object, and considering his case. It was evident that hard words would not do, for I had it on my mind that his own thoughts about himself were harder and more cutting, than anything that anyone else could say to him. Will words of God's kindness, I asked myself, and God's good news to sinners do for such a man? I determined, in dependence on God to go and try.

So one wet morning when I thought he could not be very busy, I called to pay Billy a visit. When I had set down my dripping umbrella, "Ah Billy," said I, "I am glad to see you at home; I want to have a talk with you."

He rose up from his settle in the chimney corner immediately, and said, "Can't stop—I'm busy—I must go;" and so saying he proceeded towards the door.

"But, Billy, it is raining quite hard!"

"Can't help that," said he, "we must do our work," and so he slammed the door after him and departed.

His wife made all kinds of apologies for him, because he was a very singular kind of man; he did not mean bad, but he was that curious that he said and did curious things.

After the lapse of nearly a quarter of an hour, which no doubt seemed longer to him than to me, Billy lifted the latch quietly and whispered to his wife: "The parson gone, is he?"

"No," said I; "Billy, here I am, come in."

He came in looking confused.

"Sit down, Billy, sit down; you are come to see me now. What do you want with me?"

"I don't want anything," said he, in a curt way.

"Oh yes, you do; you want a great many things, and you know you do."

He did not speak.   Then after a pause I said,

"Billy, I have been thinking much about you lately; they call you a 'lost soul.'"

"What's that to you?" said he, interrupting me.

"A good deal," I answered, "because I have a message for lost people."

"I ain't so bad as all that yet," he replied.

"But you are bad enough, Billy—bad enough."

"Yes, indeed," interposed his wife; whereat he angrily cut her short by saying,

"You hold your tongue—you're no better!"

I beckoned to her to be still, and went on to say, "You are bad enough, Billy, for an old man. How old are you?"

"Seventy years."

"Well now, that's a great age, that's the age of man: threescore years and ten; it is like giving you notice to give up the key of the tabernacle.   I am afraid you have been a kind of cumberer of the ground all this time, Billy. Do you know why the good Lord has spared you for so long?"

"I can't tell," said he, getting more and more impatient.

"Well, do you know, I think I can tell you; He is such a loving and merciful God, *He wants to have mercy on you.*   You could not have better proof of it, could you?"

He did not answer, but he seemed interested, so I went on to speak of the forbearance of God towards him, and told him that the Lord's object in this was, that it should bring him to repentance.

"Your old heart is not gone past being touched with Love, is it Billy?"

He did not reply; and as he was attentive, I read to him: "Thinkest thou this, O man, that judgest them which do such things, and doest the same, that thou shalt escape the judgment of God?   Or despisest thou the riches of his goodness and forbearance and long suffering; not knowing that the goodness of God leadeth thee to repentance? But after thy hardness and impenitent heart, treasurest up unto thyself wrath, against the day of wrath, and revelation of the righteous judgment of God; who will render to every man according to his deeds!"

"Do you understand this, Billy? God can punish you, and *He will;* but He has not done it yet because He wants to have mercy on you. What a loving and merciful God He is!"

"You are a dear man," said poor Billy, involuntarily, looking kindly at me, with tears in his eyes.

"Oh," said I, "what am I? a drop in the ocean. Think what a *dear God* He is; how patient and forbearing He has been to you. He has seen you going on year after year; you must not think that He has not seen you, or that He does not care whether you do right or wrong. He cares a great deal and He bears with us, because Christ Jesus is pleading the Blood He shed to wash away sin. He is waiting for you!"

Billy was still looking into my face; I could see that his heart was moved, and that the Holy Spirit was striving with him.

"Shall I pray with you?" I asked; and as he did not refuse I knelt down and pleaded with God for poor "lost Billy," and begged for Jesus' sake that He would give him repentance and faith, and change his heart. I left a part of the text with him.

"Think," I said, "of the '*riches* of His goodness and forbearance and long-suffering;' you have been rich in heaping up wrath against yourself, rich in all kinds of sins and blasphemies and awful curses, but God has been richer in mercy than you in rebellion, or you would have been cut down. Think of these words, and may God bless them to your soul."

The hardened old man was at last convinced and convicted too, and called upon the Lord who has promised to deliver.

God is merciful and kind, and poor old Billy was enabled to believe on Him, and was saved, and the Lord

opened the eyes of the old sinner also to see his sin, and to
hate it and avoid it. Billy did not want teaching about
the way of salvation, he had known about that from a
child; he knew that he must be converted or be lost for
ever; and he knew that God only could convert him,
therefore he never tried to save himself by works of
righteousness, or to recommend himself by making sacrifices. Satan's device with him, which had succeeded so
long, was *procrastination*, a treacherous habit which worked
on him like a spell, and held him in unwilling, yet not
unwilling, bondage; he could not do what he would, and
he seemed as if he could not help doing what he would
not, going on from sin to sin, from bad to worse, till it
pleased God, with kind words, to arrest him and bring
him to the actual point of surrender. Then he found
salvation to his great joy, and was not ashamed to acknowledge it openly, or afraid to praise God for His
goodness.

The words which had been spoken to him at the first
interview, turned out to be literally true, "God has
spared you to have mercy on you!" for soon after his
conversion of heart and change of life, he was laid on the
bed of his last sickness. His undermined constitution
could not bear much, so he rapidly sank, but his soul was
happy indeed, though he said he could not help looking
back with sorrow on a wasted and wicked life.

One Sunday morning I was summoned hastily to him
and started off without delay, but I was greeted with "It's
too late, he is gone!" I went in, however, to see the last
of him, and found his daughter still watching.

She said, "You are too late, he is dead!"

He was not dead, for though his eyes were glazed and
his hand was cold, he was still conscious. He said his soul
was happy and he pressed my hand in his, and evidently
in allusion to his daughter's words he said, "*not dead*—
just beginning to live—just beginning to live!" and thus
he passed away joyfully and triumphantly, a monument of
God's tender mercy and most forgiving love.

He had often prayed the swearer's prayer, asking God to damn his soul; but he did not mean that, and God would not hear it; but when he prayed for mercy, though he was tied and bound with chains of sin, in the pitifulness of His great mercy, and for the honor of Jesus, the Lord forgave him his sins.   To the Lord our God belong mercies and forgivenesses, though we have rebelled against Him.

> "Just as I am—poor, wretched, blind;
> Sight, riches, healing of the mind;
> Yea, all I need in Thee to find,
>   O Lamb of God, I come."

THE FAMILY OF FOUR.

HERE lived in a certain place a family consisting of Father, Mother, Son, and Daughter, all excellent friends, who delighted in each other's company and were quite content with their own home and home arrangements, and therefore they were not dependant on their neighbours for cheerfulness, or upon any outside attractions for amusement. They had every thing they wanted in themselves, and were, humanly speaking, a very happy family.

The parents had married early in life, and were therefore not much past their prime when their young people were grown up. The former were perhaps young still, in their tastes and employments, and perhaps the latter were somewhat a little old-fashioned in theirs, and so it turned out that they all agreed very well together, and were as we have said very good friends.

It is a pleasant sight to see parents and children good confiding friends, for too often parents keep on thinking or feeling that their children are only children still, though they are grown up; and grown-up children think or feel that their parents do not understand them, and that they themselves are very much in advance of the old folks, and know and do every thing better now than they used to know or do in other days.

It is a true saying that you cannot put old heads upon young shoulders, but still these people of whom we are writing, were wise enough to learn of one another. The parents seemed to learn the last new phase of thought and feeling from the young ones, and the young ones were wise enough to get the matured wisdom and judgment of their elders; the parents were pleased with and even proud of their children, and the children were proud of their parents, and they loved them for their kindness and consideration.

They saw eye to eye in every thing, these four people, and lived happily together, perfectly content with their own company. Their hours were regular for prayers and meals, and their occupations were not very onerous; and then came the cream of the day, the game at cards, or the rubber at whist in the evening. In winter or summer by the cheerful fire, or at the open window looking upon the bright and fragrant garden, all seemed well and comfortable. Very comfortable and well—*but*, and there must be a *but* in this changing passing world.

This world is not our home, only a place of passage, and there is a broad stream bearing us onward, onward, and onward without stopping; as the clock ticks and time passes on, so pass we—whither?

These happy folks were having their heaven here and enjoying the present, leaving the future to take care of itself when it came. Not that they were careless and godless people, oh no, they had their family prayers and their chapter, and their pew in church, in which they all regularly assembled twice every Sunday. In fact there was nothing against them, unless it was the charge of "pride," because they did not mix more with their neighbours. They were accounted proud towards others because they were good friends among themselves.

Now, why are not christian families always so united? generally speaking, they have far more reason to be so than worldly folks, yet alas, how true it is, they are often divided, mother against the daughter, and the father against the son. It may be said the worldly are at home in this world, and the christians are strangers; but surely as strangers they need to be adhering and leaning to one another more than the others. It may be urged also, and often is, that the prince of this world hinders their union, but it may be answered, that a greater Prince can promote union, and is actually praying and pleading for it. Perhaps it is our own fault; the perverseness of nature and the weakness of our flesh are the cause, though we blame the devil and the world. Too often the saddle is put on the wrong horse.

The family of four lived peaceably and happily together, and *considered one another*, not each one only self, and so their life flowed in an even stream, though unfortunately as we have hinted, it was flowing in the wrong direction. But there is this to be said for them, they did not think of it, and they did not know that they were all going wrong together. Like many other well-meaning and contented people they had no suspicion that their case was so bad and so unchristian and fatal as they afterwards discovered it to be.

It so happened that there came in the course of events, to their church, a Minister who preached not only *full* and *free* salvation as it is called, but he insisted that it must be a *present* salvation, or it was nothing yet, except for condemnation. And the minister would in an unflinching way divide the hearers then and there into two classes, and only two, not three; he called them the *saved* and the *unsaved*, or believers and unbelievers.

The united family did not quite like this, though they could not answer it; but they remained united still, if anything, more so; for they fortified one another against this assault on the old town of Mansoul. Sunday after Sunday the word dropped on the family of four just like the proverbial drop of water on the rock, which wore it away at last. From whatever text it came, there came still the inevitable and unwelcome allusion, or more direct assertion on the subject of the two classes; and on one occasion, the preacher said to those who were at home in this world:

"You may die before next Sunday, and then you will have to leave your home; whereas if you are saved, and are pilgrims here below, you will go Home when you die."

This came very close to the parties in question, and disturbed them more than they liked.

"There are three chances," said the preacher, "against the unbeliever, he may die to-night, or the Lord may come and shut the door, or He may withdraw His Holy Spirit, and then there would be, and could be no more opportunity for salvation."

Such things disturbed their thoughts and their rest at night, and often they were unhappy on Monday morning, and were more silent than usual. The daughter, who was the petted "baby" of the family, must needs speak out first; she said,

"I cannot sleep after those sermons; it is not fair to shut one up like that without any alternative; either we must be saved in his way or lost altogether. It is not a christian spirit."

The son agreed to this, and voted that they should all leave that Church, or if they did not they should have a game at cards when they came home, he was sure that would put it all out of their heads very soon.

The elders said nothing to this proposition, and so it fell to the ground for the present. But the Sunday after, whether it was that they were all more attentive, and more sensitive than usual, or that the preacher was, if anything, more personal in his appeals to the people, and seasoned his words with more salt, the family were greatly perturbed; albeit they were quite united in their opinion, and unanimously agreed, that it was not so positively necessary for every one to be born again; it might be necessary for bad immoral people, but steady, quiet people only needed advancement and progress; or if change of heart were necessary, there was no such particular hurry for it, it was such impatient zeal to wish to see results all at once.

On returning home they were not satisfied, even with their own final settlement of the question. So that when the son, who had voted for cards, brought out those devil's playthings, they set about their play and had a very interesting and exciting game, and certainly found much relief from the pressure which had been on them. So the evening passed away and they retired to rest, and had unbroken sleep, and met again in the morning quite elated with their successful expedient. Now they did not care, and it would not matter much how strongly the minister preached, they were up with him.

It is surprising what daring things people may do sometimes without any consciousness of their danger. These people evidently knew not what they were doing, and as such, we may suppose, came within the reach and compass of that notable prayer on the cross, which the Father does not forget, though sinners do.

The merciful Lord remembers whereof we are made. He knows the beguiling influence of Satan, and therefore regards the soul as a poor defenceless and helpless lamb in the power of the great lion. This accounts for His kind forbearance and patience towards us. He sees we are sinned against as well as sinning, and is willing to take the part of the weaker and deceived ones.

Several weeks passed on, and the family seemed as if a great barrier was removed from their quiet enjoyment, and peaceful domestic comfort; but one Sunday evening the daughter, instead of going home as usual, followed the preacher to his dwelling, and begged for a word of conversation. He being engaged with others transferred her to his wife in the next room. In a very short time she appeared again, and before all the people in the room, with smiles and tears, in a transport of joy, began to bless and praise God for His unspeakable mercy in saving her soul. The Lord had forgiven her sins and changed her heart, and she felt that her long-concealed burden was gone. With gladness of heart they all joined to sing

> "O happy day, that fixed my choice
>   On Thee, my Saviour and my God ;
> Well may this glowing heart rejoice,
>   And tell its raptures all abroad."

From that day, it may be added here, that she continued an earnest and devoted follower of Jesus, and a
faithful witness of His saving power.

On her return home, the cards were on the table and
all was ready, and she had only to put off her things and
sit down to play; but her face was changed as well as
her heart, and she laid her little hand on the cards with
firmness, and looking at her mother, said:

"I wonder God did not strike us all dead for sinning
against Him in this way; we have been trying to put
away His message from us Sunday after Sunday. Oh
mother, He is such a merciful God, He has saved me and
pardoned my sins, I dare not play another game as long
as I live. Those were solemn words to-night, 'I would
and ye would not'—and Jesus weeping too; oh mother,
I could not stand out against them, how could you?"

She was the loved one of the family, and there was such
a thrilling solemnity in her manner, no one dared to
plead for the game at cards, and they could not laugh at
her; but they seemed hurt and even angry with her for
being so changed, and they became sarcastic and then
reproachful. But she held to her experience, and the
argument of scripture; they were but cowards in this
contest and their consciences were on her side, and she
seemed to know it.

Their unity was now quite broken up, it seemed as if
some great calamity had happened to them. So, after a
silent supper, they were glad to retire for the night; but
they were perturbed, and not the less so, when they heard
the daughter in her chamber pleading earnestly late and
early for her parents and brother. Salvation was come to
the house, and she intreated that all in the house might
be partakers of it.

The next morning, in a more bright and more loving

way than usual, she set the Bible before her father. But somehow he could not read in the same unconcerned and customary way he used; a great trouble was upon him, their family union was broken, and their happiness was gone, so they sat to their silent breakfast as if the beloved daughter were dead instead of being as she was, raised from death to life.

One can feel for people like these under such circumstances, for they had set their affections on things below, and knew nothing yet of things above. To such we may suppose, a cheerful, and happy, and well-ordered home on earth is about the most desirable of all things, and nothing more could be needed while this remained. But the Lord, who orders for us better than we can ask or think, had another plan for this family. He had given them their happy nest, and it pleased Him in His kind providence in due time to stir it up; in order to show practically that this world should not be their resting place, and that they should not settle here as if they had reached their final home.

That first day of their breach and separation was long and miserable as could be, and the evening was worse for the happy gathering, the usual card-playing had ceased, and the most loved-one was going to a prayer meeting. She was going all alone, for none would go with her. She set out nevertheless, with a great burden of prayer on her soul for her parents and brother. Prayer was asked for a beloved father, and mother, and brother, that the Lord would change their hearts, and one pleaded earnestly for this, as if he knew all the circumstances of the case, and then another, and another.

At the close of the hour a young man was found in a corner of the room in great distress of soul, who sobbed aloud when he was discovered. It was no other than the brother, and he soon after received pardon, and went home with his sister rejoicing, though both of them were praying and feeling deeply for their parents. Well they might, for the poor parents were broken-hearted not so much on

c

account of sin as the alienation of their children. Religion
had brought a *sword*, not peace, into their house—their
once happy home.

The father was very grieved with his children for being
converted, and with bitter anguish he reproached the
minister for breaking up his family; but it came to his
turn next to yield to the Lord, and so it was, as it were
in spite of himself, in answer to the prayers of his children,
that he was saved and rejoiced with them. But how were
they all grieved for the mother. She was left behind very
lonely, very wretched and despairing. Long time she
remained in darkness, till at last light broke on her be-
nighted soul also, and thus were the family of four again
restored to unity on a more lasting basis. Now they were
bound together with heavenly, as before it had been only
earthly love. Now they were of one heart and one mind
in their house, with a promise from the Lord Himself of
no separation and no condemnation. Blessed are the
families that are so united, whether of four or more,
blessed in their warfare in earth, blessed in their temporary
parting in death, and most blessed in their joyful meeting
in glory hereafter.

Reader, are you a member of a united family? Is the
union for this world or for the next? Are you converted
yourself? and if so, have you borne your loving testimony
at home, and invited your loved ones to come and see
Jesus for themselves? There is very much encouragement *in* the scriptures, for the first who is converted in a
family, though it must be confessed that *out* of the scriptures, there is very much discouragement, for the young
convert is apt to look for sympathy where it cannot exist,
and being alone at first has to bear the whole burden of
the battle.

In the word we read that when the Lord lights a
candle, He sets it on a candlestick, that all who come into
the house may see the light; in short, that He wills that
the light should shine especially to those who are in darkness and in the shadow of death in that house. How

many there are in our privileged country sitting in darkness, that is, quite ignorant of the simple way of salvation, and how many who, understanding the way of salvation, are still content to remain sitting under the shadow of spiritual death, in an unconverted state. It was the Lord's will to send the first one of this family who was brought to Himself, to testify to the rest; she had her cross and her trial, and she had her joyful reward.

May the Lord bless this little narrative to your soul, and bring you to see your oneness with the Saviour; and then make you long and pray for the same blessing on all belonging to you.

"I thirst, but not as once I did,
  The vain delights of earth to share;
Thy wounds, Immanuel, all forbid
  That I should seek my pleasure there.

"Great Fountain of delight unknown,
  No longer sink below the brim,
• But overflow and pour me down
  A living and life-giving stream."

FORGIVENESS;

OR,

A USEFUL MISTAKE.

———>|<———

AVING knocked at a door by mistake, I made my apologies and was retreating, when I was asked by a voice from a window to come in. I complied, and having conversed about other things, ventured to ask my unknown friend if she frequented the house of God. She declared herself a very constant and attentive hearer, but it would appear she was not a *doer of the word*—not from any real unwillingness on her part, but simply from ignorance, or apathy, or want of application. Hers was a clear exemplification of the " narrow-necked bottle ! "

An Archbishop of Canterbury, called Anselm, likened general preaching to splashing water out of buckets over so many narrow-necked bottles ranged in rows; some drops found their way in now and then; but he said it needed subsequent visitation or personal conversation to pour the water into the necks of the bottles, to fill them to overflowing.

Here was a soul ready to receive the word, and having been made willing by the power of the Lord, her heart was opened by Him to receive the word, and she believed. The following Sunday she was a joyful and deeply interested hearer and worshipper too; but it grieved her to go away while the Lord's children remained behind to gather round the table of their Father. She spoke of this and asked me about it, that she also might have admission. Too gladly I bade her welcome. The table is spread for those who believe, for the body of the Lord was broken and His blood was shed on the cross for them. I said, if you repent of your sins and intend to lead another life, and are in charity with all men; by all means come, and welcome.

Week after week, however, passed by, and she came not; and I saw also her joy was failing, and her attention was becoming listless.

"What is the matter?" I asked. "Why do you not come! Do you not believe that Jesus died for your sins, and rose again for your justification?"

"Yes," she replied, "I thank God I can and do believe that."

"Is not your mind entirely changed about the past, and bent on walking before the Lord in the land of the living, for the future, by God's help?"

"Yes."

"Now what is it? Is there anything against your neighbours?"

At this she coloured and was silent.

"Are you not in charity with some one or more?"

Yet there was no answer.

"Well," I continued, "I cannot wonder at your state; but I will say this for you, I would rather have you hang back for this reason, than go on as if it were all right when it was not so. It is a bad thing not to be in charity with all men, but far worse to go on under these circumstances without feeling or caring."

She told me her mother-in-law had injured her deeply, she could not forgive her; and then she became agitated even to tears.

"No," she said, "I never will forgive her."

"Never is a long word, and does not become God's

child. You *must* forgive, and you must ask for grace to enable you to do it. How can the love of God dwell in your heart if you do not from your heart forgive your neighbour, as freely as God has forgiven you far deeper injuries done to Himself? When God forgives us, He sheds abroad His love in our hearts by the Holy Spirit which is given, and you should show this love, that it is essentially a *forgiving love;* it assures you forgiveness, and it urges you to forgive those who have injured you."

"No," she said, "I cannot—it is no use—I cannot forgive her."

"Come now, let us kneel down and tell God that you have such a strong animosity against your relative, that you cannot forgive her. He can subdue the unruly will, and all sinful affections. Shall we kneel?"

After a long silent struggle she knelt, and we made this confession to God, and pleaded for grace to enable her to overcome, but there was no response. Again we pleaded for grace, and at last came the "amen," and with it tears of anguish; but the recollections of the injury and the grievance seemed to rise up like a flood, and sweep all good resolves away; and she rose from her knees declaring it was no use—it could not be.

Again we knelt and prayed, and she interrupted me with saying, "What am I to do? Am I to go to her and tell her I forgive her? I cannot—I will not."

"Well," I said, "you must consider it well and prayerfully; I think you will lose far more than you gain by this unavailing revenge and animosity."

A few days after I came again, and found her not unwilling to open the subject, and I found that she had done and said enough for her part to ask her mother-in-law's forgiveness for herself. I was led, therefore, to put the matter in this way:

"Suppose you go to the house and see her, and ask her to forgive you because the Lord has forgiven you."

"No," she said, "this is harder than the other."

"Well, but let us begin with the hardest first. Shall

we again pray to God to help you, and will you set off at once, and not parley with yourself any longer? How much joy and liberty you lose, and for what? What do you get by harbouring this unforgiving spirit in your heart?"

After prayer she rose, and said she would go.

"But when? Go at once, don't delay; the great secret of victory in such trying conflicts, is promptness. Go off now."

She assented, to my great joy, and putting on her bonnet and cloak, proceeded at once, promising to come and tell me the result. Hour after hour passed away, and yet she came not, and I feared her resolution had failed her.

The next day I went to enquire, and found that she had been there, but that as she approached the gate her heart beat so violently that she could not go in, so she passed it and then turned and returned, but it was of no use, she could not go in.

"Shall I go with you?"

"No," she replied, thanking me, "no—*by God's help I will go*, and I will conquer this feeling!"

We thanked God for this token of victory, and I bid her take courage, and come to me after the dreaded interview.

She made another attempt, and was able to open the gate and walk up the once familiar path where she had not been for more than two years, and with trembling hand she knocked at the door. She was admitted and shewn into the adjoining room, where she was at once confronted with her mother-in-law. In mutual surprise they looked at one another till the daughter-in-law burst into tears and said,

"Mother, will you forgive me?"

After a moment's pause they were silently locked in a mutual embrace, and the mother said,

"My dear, I think I have more need to ask your forgiveness; will you forgive me?"

Oh the joy of such reconciliation! If they had not really loved one another, they could not have retained mutual jealousies and wounded feelings; they would have grown indifferent to one another; but now that they were reconciled again, their love gushed up with more abundant flow, and they became greater friends than ever.

Her happiness and her joyful thankfulness to the God of all grace abounded more and more, and with swelling heart she came for the first time to her place at the Lord's table. It was a bright and happy day, only surpassed by that in which she had the joy of leading her mother to Jesus, and the privilege of rejoicing with Him for having found her, the wandering sheep which had been lost.

"Be ye kind one to another, tender-hearted, forgiving one another, even as God for Christ's sake has forgiven you." *Eph.* iv. 32. "Be ye therefore followers of God as dear children." *Eph.* v. 1.

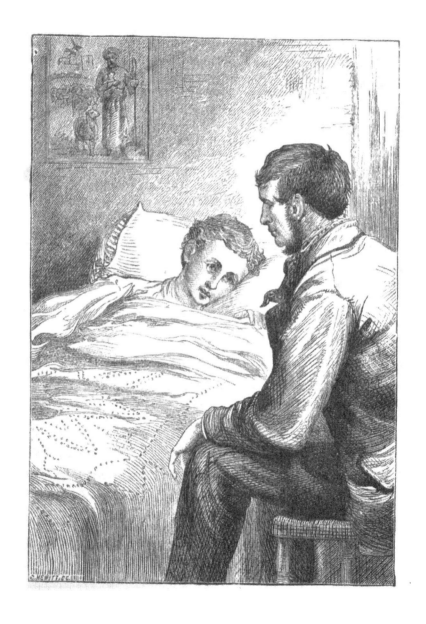

THE NINES AND SIXES

T was a bright glowing evening, the sun was quietly setting in the sea, and a path of burnished gold seemed to lead to the place; while the great clouds above, which, for a time, had darkened the sun, were now gilded by it, and most glorious to behold.

On a low pallet lay a poor young sufferer, a lad, who had passed through much pain of body, and many conflicts of doubt in his mind. Fearfulness and trembling had been upon him, and horror had overwhelmed him; his heart had been sore pained within him, and the terrors of death had fallen on him; often he had been tempted to wish, "O that I had wings like a dove! for then would I fly away, and be at rest: I would escape."

But how then would the merciful chastening of a loving Father have had its required effect? Then at times, he had wished that the enemy that had done this might be destroyed; but even then, would the chastening have been in vain. At length, he saw the hand of the Lord, and heard His voice, which said, "Cast thy burden upon the Lord, and He shall sustain thee!" His soul then rested in peace, and the heavy dark clouds, which had so pressed upon him, became like those above the sunset, bright and golden, with the light of a heavenly Father's love shining on them. All was calm now; the time of the boy's departure was at hand; and he was looking for it, as he had been hitherto for the coming of the Lord.

"Will you meet me in heaven?" said the lad to his father, looking anxiously and steadily, as if he expected a definite answer from him; but receiving none, he again ventured to repeat his question: "Father, will you promise to meet me in heaven?"

"My dear son, how gladly would I meet you; I hope I may, for I do desire to be with the Lord."

"Don't speak like that, father; *turn the nines into sixes*, will you?"

"What do you mean, my boy?" said the man, looking earnestly into his son's face; "what nines do you mean?"

"Oh, father, I used to go on wishing and hoping like that for a long time, but I got nothing by it, so I turned my wishes into real prayers at last, and God answered me; then it came to my mind, and I remembered about it, how the figure 9 is one that points downwards, just like good desires which come from heaven; and I thought if we turn that figure up the other way it makes a 6; that is just like turning the good desires God gives us into prayers to Him. He tells us to call upon Him in the day of trouble, and He says, He will deliver us, and we shall glorify Him. Wishing did not do me any good; it was just like writing a letter without any direction, and I got no answer to it, the devil was all the time cheating me out of my opportunity of believing on the Lord; time was passing away, and I was not ready to go, so I began to pray to God to save my soul: I said, 'Oh Lord, I beseech Thee, deliver my soul.'"

The father still persisted in wishing and hoping; but the son equally persisted in getting beyond that, and he got his father to make a promise that he would pray.

"When will you pray, father? *Pray now!*" said the boy, beseechingly—"pray now! turn your desires into prayers now, father. Let me pray with you before I go away."

The father knelt down, but he found it difficult to make a particular and definite request, because the desires he professed to have were so general. Feeling the vagueness of his state, he cried, "O Lord, help me! O Lord, teach me! O, make me a real Christian! Lord, save my soul! have mercy on me, a sinner!"

The dying boy was all this time rejoicing in his soul, as all do who have received answer from God themselves, and who know therefore, from their own experience, how willing and ready God is to hear and answer prayer. The man had begun, and opened a direct communication between his soul and the unseen God. It was not likely that the Lord would refuse the prayer; and in due time it was answered, and the father and son were permitted to rejoice together.

The father was converted; the Lord had been gracious to him, and had delivered his eyes from tears, his feet from falling, and his soul from death; but not without first opening his eyes, to show him the sinfulness of himself and his sins. The Lord made him feel the sorrows of death; that is, the sorrow of separation from God. Oh, how many there are who know they are separate from God, and have no direct communication with Him; who yet have no sorrow about it, but who rather think they may rejoice in the world all the more for feeling no restraint. They have a *void*, and feel it too, sometimes; but it is not an *aching void*, and so much the more is the pity.

The sorrows of death precede the joys of life. No wonder the angels rejoice over sinners repenting, for they know why the Lord opens the eyes of men to see themselves; and why He makes them mourn for their sins, and feel the darkness of being without God; it is that He may draw them to Himself, who is *the Light*, that He may deliver them from the power of Satan to Himself, in order that they may have forgiveness of sins and an inheritance among them that are sanctified by faith, which is in Jesus Christ.

To those who know and feel what it is *to be saved*, it is a matter of great uneasiness, to say the least of it, to see their beloved ones still unsaved—still Christless and hopeless; and all the more miserable are they when their unsaved ones are buoying themselves up with hopes and intentions, or works of righteousness which they are doing, instead of *sinking down* as helpless drowning men, to be saved by One who alone can deliver them, and bring them to a place of safety, and pardon, and peace, and rejoicing.

The dying boy was permitted to rejoice with his father; for now they could sympathise with one another, and understand one another, as only those can who have actual experience of salvation. Soon after, peacefully and joyfully, the soul of the boy departed to be at rest, and to wait in another state for that time, when we shall wake up in the Lord's likeness in body as well as soul, and be satisfied with it.

Can we not learn a good lesson from the boy's "nines and sixes?" How many there are who have not got beyond hoping, and are actually resting on their good intentions; they little suspect how God regards them, and how surely their good desires will rise up as God's witnesses against them hereafter; for they come from God and are intended to urge them to *act now* on His word. What could our God do more for us than to give His only Son to die for our sins, and to raise Him up for our justification, and to send us His word of salvation, and above all, to give us His Holy Spirit to come and strive with us in our hearts—by these good desires? With some the Spirit strives in their consciences, by making them feel they *ought* to yield themselves to God; but we are speaking now of persons who are directly under the drawings of the Holy Spirit, by good *desires*, and sometimes by intense yearnings for salvation. Oh that such would at once turn their "nines into sixes"—for nothing is simpler, if between their souls and their God alone, where there is no one to criticise, or distract, or disturb them, they would deliberately and intentionally turn the wishes which God has put into their hearts into prayers to God. Could He, would He give such desires, if He were not willing to fulfil them?

Reader, do you really desire to *serve the Lord?* I will not ask, do you wish to be saved, for that desire may spring from natural causes, and be only the selfish moving of a heart that fears to go to hell—but do you desire to be a servant of God? Know you not that to whom we yield ourselves servants to obey, his servants we are to whom we obey, whether of sin unto death, or obedience unto righteousness.

Do you really desire to *serve* the Lord? then, behold, the word of the Lord says to thee, Choose you, *this day*, whom you will serve; do not halt between two opinions, but do what no one else can do for you, and what you must do for your own self, or perish! *Choose*—present to yourself to the Lord, as one who desires to serve Him. Lord, I will serve Thee. The God who loves the cheerful giver, the Lord who narrowly observes the actions of men, will not overlook you, *be sure* of it. Beg Him to send the fire of the Spirit, to fix your choice, and make you His for ever. Turn the "nines into sixes!"

We never repent of doing this; to the world it may appear like a "losing concern," as they would say; but to us it is better thus to lose, that we may gain hereafter, than to gain all the world now, with all its pleasure, and lose our own souls at last. If hoping and wishing people only knew how near they are to the object of their desires, there would be fewer of them.

When a man professes that he wishes and hopes to be saved, he seems to acknowledge two things: first, that he is not saved; secondly, that God is striving with him, and moreover that he has not yet yielded himself to that striving. Can anything aggravate more the sin and danger of such a man? Strange to say, in this hoping there is a delusive spell, a kind of enchantment, which flatters a man and causes him to think that his case is not so bad. It is said the road to hell is paved with good intentions! Is it not sad that men should neglect and

forsake the road to heaven, which has been made at a
tremendous sacrifice, and make a way for themselves to
hell, a place which was never intended for them?

See a gang of convicts in their clanking chains,
making a road to the sea. In this you see a picture of
such as refuse present salvation, and preferring darkness
to light, lend themselves to a cruel and unrelenting
master, who employs them in this manner, to make their
own way to destruction. The hope which comes before
faith is not from God, but from the devil. God's hope is
given after faith. It is given to believers only, and is
sure and everlasting; an anchor of the soul.

When good desires are given, whether to sinners for
salvation, or to believers for edification and advancement,
it is, as we have before said, on purpose that they may be
turned into prayers. Surely these good desires are the
tokens of God's gracious purposes towards us, which He
is waiting to accomplish. He does not intend that we
should work them out, but rather surrender ourselves
willingly to Him, that He may do so. Again, these
desires are, as it were, the voice of God Himself speaking
to us, and we should at once and readily respond to it if
we would obtain the benefits proffered to us.

We have an interesting instance of turning nines into
sixes in the twenty-seventh Psalm. Speaking of the
blessedness of the Lord's presence, the Psalmist goes on
to shew how he attained the privilege of dwelling in it
continually. In the eighth verse we read, " When Thou
saidst, Seek ye my face; my heart said unto Thee, Thy face,
Lord, will I seek."

It will be observed how close he keeps to the words of
the offer which is made to him. He simply reverses the
words which are spoken.

The voice of God says, Seek ye My face; his response is,
Thy face, Lord, will I seek. It is useful to notice this,
for whether it is in words of promise written, or by
thoughts and desires suggested to the mind, God still
speaks to us, and assuredly it is our wisdom to fall in with

the very word and thought suggested, and to adopt it as our prayer.

The point to notice first is, that the Psalmist keeps close to the word; secondly, that he acts promptly and without hesitation—when Thou saidst, then I said. This is a great secret of success in our transaction with God to be prompt, and to act at once, before Satan has time to suggest procrastination to some more convenient season.

The third point to be mentioned in this verse, is the directness with which the response is made to the Lord Himself; Thy face, Lord, will I seek. He speaks not as to a third person, or as if of an absent one. Prayer is a direct appeal to a present person for a certain thing.

Lastly, it is all done from the heart; "My heart said said unto Thee." Thus we may say, wishes should be turned into prayer literally, promptly, directly, and heartily; and there can be no doubt that the answer intended will not long be delayed.

Then in conclusion, let it be suggested that when the answer is given, an equally direct and hearty acknowledgment should be made in thanksgiving. It is a good thing to be thankful, better still to give thanks.

How many persons stop at this point of hoping and wishing? or if they pass this barrier, they stop short at the next, that of giving thanks. Numbers of persons are hindered and kept in bondage by this common mistake. They deprive themselves of liberty, because they restrain thanksgiving. The command is, "In every thing give thanks;" not be grateful only, but give thanks, for this is the will of God in Christ Jesus concerning you.

THE ELECT;

OR

VIEWS OF HIS OWN.

AN earnest and a zealous man was J. M——, and very eager for conversation on religious matters, for he had some views of his own which he loved to tell and to battle for. He said he was one of the elect, because he knew he was, and was quite sure of it! No one wished to doubt his assertion, and no one cared to grudge him the honor and privilege he claimed for himself, rather they would rejoice with him; but why should he speak of it as if it were a matter of contention?

"Why?" asked John, "because people don't believe it, they are so ignorant about the true doctrines of grace."

"That is a reason why you should speak gently and persuasively; you can afford to be quiet and firm, for you have nothing to lose."

"But people are always so contrary; they do not know what it is themselves, and will not believe that any body can be elect."

"It takes two people to make a controversy, and if you will not be one, you will have no occasion to complain."

"May I ask you what makes you think you are one of the elect? I hope you are, I am sure, and I trust it may really prove so, but how do you know? If a wolf went about saying, I am a lamb, I am a lamb, I do not think it would prove it, but rather the reverse, for lambs appear as they are, and people who have any sense can see the fact for themselves."

"I was sitting under the word one day," replied John, "when it came to my mind with great power from the Lord, it was, I am sure of it—I will never doubt it—no one can make me doubt it."

Seeing my incredulity, or what he thought was such, he began to rate me for being as bad as other people.

"Oh for that, I am not only as bad, but as far as I know I am worse; but I think the scripture says that those whom the Lord elects are predestinated, and He calls them and justifies them. Are you justified yet?"

"No, but I shall be, I am sure I shall."

"Then you have not received justification yet. They say it takes some thousands of years for the light of some stars to reach the earth, though light travels at a wonderful rate. For what we know there may be a great many great stars whose light, though it has been travelling for ages, has not yet reached us; but you know till the light does reach and appear to us, we cannot know about those stars. God knows them of course, and they are real stars, but they are not *stars to us yet.* God may have elected you before the foundation of the world, but how am I to know it till you are justified? There are certain marks by which you know the elect; they are made manifest by a remarkable change which takes place in them, for they are changed from wolf to lamb, from Adam to Christ—Are you?"

"No," he replied, "not yet, but you will never put me out of it."

"I do not wish to put you out of it, I want to put you in the way of knowing it for certain, and showing others the reality of the fact. God does not tell us we are elect, but rather first He shews us by His Holy Spirit, what we are by nature—that we are sinners and even lost sinners. This is the first work of the Spirit; to convince of sin. He has various ways by which He brings us to this knowledge. Sometimes by directly convicting us; sometimes by shewing us His goodness and melting us to submission; and sometimes by revealing His kind purposes toward us, thus overcoming us by His love. But in all these and many other ways, He intends to bring us first to see ourselves, so that we *abhor self* and *repent in dust and ashes,* and then He reveals Himself to us as a pardoning Lord and gives us ' His seal.' "

He was unconvinced still and full of dispute, but he could not rest, elect as he professed to be ; . he was restless as if he were not content with the "seal of the Lord" which he said he had. After many weeks he came again one Sunday evening to converse, but this time in a different spirit. Instead of coming to tell me his meaning of some text, he came to ask *the* meaning, evidently troubled about his soul.

" I have read in a book, John, that the elect are *whosoever will,* and the non-elect are *whosoever will not* come to Jesus ! " This was rather too much for John, for he could not stand "freewillers," he had heard that freewillers tore up God's covenant and threw it in His face. He did not like freewillers at all.

" Well, John, the matter is very simple and clear ; there is a mark by which we may know the elect of God, and when I do not see the mark I cannot say a man will never have it ; nay, I rather hope and desire he may, but till he has it, I must withhold the word. My name may be down in a church register for a Christian, but till I have true repentance towards God and true faith towards the Lord Jesus Christ, I am not a real Christian yet as I should be."

John went away unable to reply and unwilling to yield, but evidently uneasy and unhappy. At the end of the week he appeared again, and said he had been praying and trying very hard to feel that repentance and faith which I had mentioned.

" John, you can never feel a thing till you have it ; you will not get it by feeling it, though you will feel it when you get it. People often profess to believe that God will save them—they believe God's promises, but they should begin with receiving the word which He is saying to them, and which refers to them now in their present state, instead of the word which may refer hereafter. Now, at this time God's word does not say to you, I will save you some day, but it says you are a sinner, tied and bound with chains which you cannot break; it says 'the wrath of God is on you because you do not believe on the name of the Son of God;' it says, that you are now actually under *condemnation!* When a man believes this you soon see what effect it has upon him; how his mind, and his plans, and his arguments, are all changed; for, instead of contending that he is a Christian elected from eternity to eternity, he cries from his inmost soul, 'God be merciful to me a sinner;' 'Lord, save me, I perish.' This is a very different story to 'Lord, I thank Thee that I am not as other men are!' A man who has once felt the convicting power of God cannot rest till he has also felt His pardoning love, and then he begins to praise God as distinctly as before he began to cry to Him for mercy."

"This is the Spirit's work in our souls by which we are awakened to see ourselves and our danger, and then brought to see the great salvation which has been provided for us in Christ Jesus. Do you understand this?"

John went away, convinced this time that he had been "building on a wrong token," and soon after he began to get more and more miserable. Sometimes he was impatient, and sometimes he was despairing; sometimes he thought hard things of religion and all religious people, and then that he had made a great mistake in giving up his past religious profession; sometimes he thought God was very hard toward him, and sometimes that God would never, never, cast him off. Poor man, he was sorely bewildered, and perplexed, and could not rest anywhere. He determined not to go the voyage with his vessel this week, and then he was wretched because the vessel was gone away without him.

Now fairly at his wits' end he tried to pray, but he could

not, and then he took up the Testament, and his eyes fell
on the words, "Come unto me, all ye that labour and are
heavy laden." He felt as if the Lord were speaking those
words to him, his heart seemed to melt at the thought
that the Lord was feeling for him and sorry for him, and
his weary labourings. He did not say, I have elected you
and will come and fetch you, stay where you are; but
" *Come unto Me and I will give you rest.*" It was not—come
to the true doctrines, or come to My minister, or come to
My church, but come unto Me—a present, personal
Saviour, a loving, living Person, who has been striving
with you. John *came to Jesus* as he was, weary, and
worn, and sad; and he did not come in vain, for virtue
came from Jesus and saved his soul, and made him truly
happy.

John was now a very different man to what he had
been, and he got true rest, not from believing in *election*,
but in something nearer, namely, the *finished work of
Christ.* He rested because his Saviour had done all that
was needful for his salvation, and now he knew that he
was one of the elect, for the Lord would not have converted and saved him if it were otherwise. It was very
clear, and John was exceedingly happy, and he thought
and said that nothing should ever again shake his confidence; it was quite impossible that he could doubt any
more. But, poor man, he had yet to learn that his conflicts were not all over, though his unreasonable labours
to obtain rest were; he had yet to learn that he must take
up the Lord's yoke and follow Him, and thus find another
rest which he had not attained yet.

We have rest from works to obtain salvation given to
us when we believe in Jesus the Saviour, who died and
rose again; but in order to find that rest which enables
us to follow Him peacefully, we must submit ourselves,
and yield our will entirely to Him.

Like all young converts, John came into conflicts and
doubts about his final security; he used to think at times
that he would surely be lost after all!

"John," said his friend to him, "your business in that steamer is down below in the engine room; you cannot see which way the vessel is going, you may be driving the engine full speed, right upon rocks, or backing into danger, but you are not disturbed in your mind down there about that. You know in this harbour there is a dangerous bar of sand, very few know the channel, and a mistake might upset the vessel and you too far inside to get out; are you not troubled about that?"

"Oh no," said John, cheerfully, "don't you see our captain knows the channel, and the bars, and the rocks, and all—very few better than he; I never trouble about that!"

"Just so, John, if you would trust the great Pilot to order you and guide you with His eye, I don't think you would ever miss your way; and I am sure if you trusted your soul with Him, as you do your life with your captain, you would 'not trouble at all," but find such a sweet peace and rest in Him. The world cannot give such rest, and what is more, the world cannot take it away."

John was enlightened, and the next time his friend went to the vessel to see her start on her voyage, all was hurry and bustle, the escaping steam was making a loud harsh noise, the bell was ringing, and now and then the deafening shrill whistle was sounded to clear the way. John was standing at the head of the companion ladder, and when he caught his friend's attention, he patted his own breast with happy satisfaction, and pointed to the steady old captain who was standing on the paddlebox bridge, signifying by the sign, "He is in his place, and I am not afraid;" and he meant more than this! He seemed to say, "The Lord is my Shepherd, I shall not want."

So John holds on his way rejoicing and resting, going on to that other rest, which remaineth for the people of God in His glory.

JESUS! the sinner's Friend,
   We hide ourselves in Thee!
God looks upon Thy sprinkled blood;
   It is our only plea.

He hears Thy precious name;
We claim it as our own;
The Father must accept and bless
   His well-belovèd Son.

He sees Thy spotless robe;
Thy blood has cancelled sin;
The golden gates have welcomed Thee,
   And we may enter in.

Jesus! the sinner's Friend,
We cannot speak Thy praise;
No mortal voice can sing the song,
   That ransomed hearts would raise.

THE BETHEL FLAG.

A LADY, whose husband was a prosperous and wealthy man, was sitting one day in her house, employed as usual about some fancy work of taste and skill, to while away her time. She had no family to occupy her thoughts and anxieties, and therefore had plenty of leisure; and she had also plenty of means and every desire to do good to her neighbours, but she did not know what to do or how to do it.

She gladly relieved the poor when they came to her with the tale of want and sorrow, and kindly took some little comforts for the sick and suffering ones about her. She had not yet been awakened to see her own state, or to care for her own soul, and therefore spiritual kindness to others was unknown to her; and, besides, she had some vague idea, that it was the minister's work exclusively to care for the souls of the people, just as it was the doctor's to heal the body when afflicted. She did not know that she was expected to be "her brother's keeper," and never thought that anything more was required of her in her position of influence than what she did.

The servant announced to her that, Sam the sailor wished to see her. "Bring him here," was the cheerful and ready answer. And so Sam, the veritable Sam, stood before her.

This said Sam was a great character in his way, and a good faithful seaman, though he had been a very daring wicked man. A marvellous change had come over him, and he was now the subject of much wonder and talk. People were amazed to see such a lion changed into such a lamb; such a hardy, daring sailor, turned into such a tender-hearted, conscientious man, who was happy all the day, fearlessly rebuking vice and swearing, and caring for the souls of his shipmates and others.

His captain observed his consistency and spirituality, and was much edified by it, and spoke often of him with much feeling. Sam became first mate in his master's vessel, and was always on the look-out, not only for his owner's benefit, as he was bound to do, but for the Lord's work, and to do good to the souls of his fellow-seamen.

In this respect he was a contrast to the lady. They both had the will to do good: she had worldly influence, but he had spiritual power; she was amiable, kind, and moral; he the reverse of all this, but changed at last and brought to usefulness and blessing.

Whenever the ship was at anchor and secure in port, Sam made it a rule to send round to other vessels to collect men together for prayer and praise. He could not read much himself, and therefore he was dependent on one of his invited company, if any one could, to read a few verses from the Testament, and then Sam gave his testimony for the Lord, in his own sailor-like way, and spoke of his past life and sins with tears, and of the Lord's goodness to him in saving his soul. Thus he recommended the Saviour and forgiving God to his audience. He was well known, and his vessel was looked for by many, and hailed with gladness when she hove in sight; though of course, some regarded him in a different light, and thought him mad or silly; and sometimes they treated him with contempt, not to say more. But he was always well and happy, and did not vex himself much about the opposition of the unruly.

It came to his mind to have a *Bethel Flag*, for occasions

when there was leisure and liberty to hold a service on board the well-known ship.

"Nothing," said Sam, "gets on without first praying about it. We may just as well leave a thing undone, if it is not worth praying about."

People very often think what they will do and how they will do it; but after all, the Lord works it all in His own way, and not in ours; or He does not do it, or suffer it to be done. We may as well consult with Him first. "Make a rule and always keep to it, to pray about a thing before doing it."

Sam prayed about the flag, if it was the Lord's will, he should like to have such a thing. The price of it, however, was far beyond any resources within his reach; but it came to his mind one day, as if by chance, just like a stray thought, to go and ask "Missus." The owner's kind wife was well known among the sailors as well as their families; he determined accordingly to go and see "Missus," and was in due course shown into her presence.

The drawing-room, where the lady was sitting, was a spacious, elegant apartment. Poor Sam began to feel, he did not know how—it was "making so bold," and he almost wished he had not come; but the lady kindly reassured him, and said,

"Well, Sam, I am glad to see you; what can I do for you?"

The man was taken aback, and made his bow and twirled his cap, and made apologies; and if you please, mum, he would very much like to have a Bethel Flag for the ship, if her honour would be so kind.

"What's a Bethel Flag, Sam?"

"A blue flag with a white dove on it, mum, to hoist at the masthead when we have leisure for a meeting aboard. We have had some blessed meetings on board she ship, mum."

"You shall have it, Sam. How large will you have it?"

Sam was rather put about by this question, for he had

not yet thought of such a detail of the plan as this. He was perplexed for a little, and then looking round the room, he said,

"As big as the room, mum."

"Very well, Sam, go and order it."

Sam would have said "Thank ye, mum," in his own hearty and happy way; but the room was very large, and there was no need for so much expense, and therefore he muttered something about the size of the room.

"How large is it, Sam?   Measure it."

He did so, with his paces, and reckoned it twenty-eight by eighteen feet.

"Is that large enough?" said the lady. "Have it, Sam, and may you do much good with it."

"Thank you, mum, and the Lord bless you for it, and for all the good that is done under it when it's a-flying."

Poor Sam made a hasty exit, for the tears came into his eyes, and into the lady's too, for Sam spoke kindly from his heart, and touched her heart as well.

Sam went forth, thanking the Lord, and ordered his flag twenty-eight feet by eighteen feet, and in due time got it; but while it was preparing, it came to Sam's heart that he would have a preaching on board his ship when the flag was first hoisted. So he went and made bold to ask the minister, who readily promised to attend on a certain Sunday afternoon, at three o'clock.

In due course, at the appointed time, a great concourse of people were assembled to witness the unfurling of the Bethel Flag. An appropriate hymn was given out, and then there was a pause while Sam hoisted his great flag in the presence of the people, in the shape of a ball, right up to the mainmast head.   There it remained in that manner during the singing of the hymn and the subsequent prayer, and then when the text was given out, Sam stood by to pull the halyard and let the flag fly out in all its grand proportions; the gigantic dove, and the great olive branch, and the word "Bethel" in big letters, each more than three feet high.

The text was from Genesis xxviii. 19, and the minister spoke of the poor desolate young man, Jacob, who was fleeing from his home, and fleeing for his life, a stranger alone in a strange land, weary and homeless; and how the Lord had compassion on him, for he knew his father and his father's father—they were the Lord's friends; and for their sakes He came to do good to the poor young man. He let him have some refreshing sleep, and shewed him a beautiful and wonderful vision in a dream—"a ladder set up on the earth, whose top reached to heaven, and behold the angels of God were ascending and descending upon it; and behold, the Lord stood above and said, I am the Lord God of Abraham thy father, and the God of Isaac; the land whereon thou liest, to thee will I give it, and to thy seed; and behold, I am with thee, and will keep thee in all places whither thou goest." When Jacob awaked from his sleep, he said, "Surely the Lord is in this place; this is none other than the house of God, the gate of heaven, and he called the name of that place *Bethel.*" Jacob believed the word, and took the stone which he had for his pillow, and set it up for a pillar, a mark of possession. The place where the word of God reaches a soul effectually, is its Bethel, the gate through which it enters into the way of life and happiness; we should have faith, and mark the day, the place, and the word.

Reader, do you know of a Bethel? Has the word of the Lord ever come effectually to you? Look well to it, for it will be a solemn thing if no such transaction has ever taken place between your soul and God.

The minister then appealed to the many people attracted by that flag, and begged that many might there and then receive a word from God under it, particularly that the Lord would meet with some wandering ones, whom He cares for, for their fathers' and their mothers' sake; some children, whom praying parents had held up before God with faith for a long while. He entreated that if any were there, they would come forward and yield themselves to the Lord at once and pray, or ask for faith, that they might believe in the Lord to the salvation of their souls.

Several came forward, and believing, rejoiced, and that day there was joy in heaven in the presence of the angels of God over sinners repenting. One does not see all the Lord's work; only some of it is permitted to come into sight, and sometimes we hear of more afterwards. There was one that day, not the child of praying parents, but the word struck him in a reverse way. He was the un-praying father of praying children, a conscience-stricken wanderer. The word reached him as he stood in the distance, to all appearance perfectly indifferent to the proceedings. He heard the flutter of the flag, and he heard the words of the speaker, and then walked quietly away towards his house, not deigning to look round till he reached his door; and then when he did turn to look, the flag was hauled down, and the service was over.

Something smote him now with a gloomy dejection, and he sat down in his house, and said, "Is the offer past? Have I refused it again? Must I perish?" His wife could say nothing to console him, for she was very much in the same way herself, and for fear of him she had been restrained from seeking the Lord. He came into great trouble of mind, and he never rested till he found peace with God. Then he, with his son and daughter, could not rest till his wife was converted also.

Since that day, that Bethel Flag has fluttered over many from time to time, who have been blessed of God under His preached word, and dear Sam's prayer and labour of faith have not been in vain. But with all his encouragements, his heart yearned for the generous donor of the flag, and it is hoped, not in vain.

Wherever there is a kind will to do good, and it is exercised, the Lord accepts it and owns it, and does never forget the work and labour which is done for His people or His name; but surely, it is a pity to do good to others and have nothing of it ourselves. How sad and grievous to help to build the ark for others, and to be eventually lost ourselves.

May the Lord bless this little tale to some kind souls who love to do good, and are themselves without it, that they also may be blessed; and may the good Lord bless it to poor wandering ones, who are the objects of earnest prayer and solicitude.

WHAT A SHAME.

VISITING among cottages one day, I came to one where a woman was in great trouble about her sick child which was dangerously ill. It seemed to be hovering between death and life. The doctor had just been there and had given no hope of recovery, but he said that children do recover in a marvellous way; and to this slender prospect the mother's heart clung.

"Will God spare my child?" she asked with an anxious look.

"Have you asked Him?" I enquired; "have you prayed to Him?"

This was just what she had not done; she had only hoped and feared.

"Do not rest in hopes or be deterred by fears, but pray and trust in God."

The Lord heard and answered the mother's prayer, and in due time the child was restored; but while we were praying, her husband came in, clattered the chairs about, and manifested his impatience in many ways, though without any positive effort to stop the prayer. When we rose from our knees, he was standing in the middle of the room, with his hat on his head, and his hands in his pockets, half turning away from us; he presently looked up and said,

"Do you think that is any good? do you think your prayer can do good when the doctor's medicine has failed? It's all superstition and nonsense!"

"Our prayers," I replied, "cannot, but God can! Jesus promised if two of you shall agree to ask—"

"I don't believe a word of such stuff," said he angrily; "you are paid for talking like this, but I don't think you believe it either—do you now?" said he, turning to me, as if he had fairly detected me in a trick of trade!

"I have read of such people as you," I replied, "but I do not often meet with such; I should like to have a talk with you very much. You have told me what you do not believe, I should like to know what you do believe."

"I believe," he said, "I want my dinner now; it's all very well for you who have nothing to do; working makes a man hungry. Now then, Betsy, let's have the dinner; be quick;" so saying, he sat down in his chair while his wife bustled about to get the dinner, and I retired, promising to come in the evening for a talk, and telling him I hoped he would not run out of the way.

It is needless to narrate all the conversation which took place that evening. The man was very ignorant and self-opiniated; but he admitted that Jesus Christ had been into this world, and had died upon the cross, though he did not know why or what he himself had to do with it. He admitted that Jesus Christ would come again to this world; but even on this head he did not know what would be the effect on him; he had never applied these and such like facts to himself. I shewed him from Scripture that Jesus came as the "Lamb of God." That just as the Jews brought a lamb that had not sinned to die in the place of the sinner who had, (because without shedding of blood there could be no remission,) so God provided His own Son to be the substituted sacrifice for the sins of all men. And now since that blood had been shed, *there is remission* for all who believe and shew their faith by coming to Jesus for the remission of their sins.

He did not answer or reason, but seemed rather disposed to yield to reason, and we then parted with prayer, he promising me that he would come to church next Sunday. Joseph was full of his going to church; he had not been there since he went to be married, except once to the funeral of a friend of his. So when Sunday arrived, about half an hour before the service time, Joseph put on, not his Sunday, but his "best coat," which was rather tight and irksome; and while he was standing before the chimney glass and adjusting it, some of his usual companions happened to look in at the window. They watched him for some time, and then one of them exclaimed,

"Look there! I do believe Joseph is going to church!" and they all roared with laughter, and came rushing into the house, making great fun. Poor Joseph's resolution fled like smoke before the wind.

"Church! going to church! what will you think of next?" said he; "I am going by train!" (his wife was dismayed at the ready lie,) the clock was wrong, and the train was gone, he should go now and shift his clothes. And so he did, and he went and spent the day on the beach with his companions, albeit with a bad conscience.

Not seeing Joseph at church, according to promise, I called on him the next morning and heard the sad tale, and found him very dejected and ashamed of himself.

"I won't scold you, Joseph, but will you be a man next Sunday, and keep your word, and not be ashamed to come?"

"If I do live," said he, in a very determined manner.

"Very good," said I, offering my hand.

The next Sunday he was true to his word and came, but he had risen early, and two hours before church time, had left his home, dressed in his best, setting out in the opposite direction, for fear any inquisitive neighbours should think he was going to church. He walked round through a wood, and came out a long way on the other side beyond the church, and then walked along the road as if he were going home, and just stepped in with other people into the church and sat down. When once there, he was afraid to look about, for he felt as if everybody was looking at him, and wondering to see him there.

After the service was over, Joseph was greatly pleased with himself for having kept his resolution, and he promised to come again in the evening. One of his working companions hearing this, invited him to a prayer meeting in the afternoon.

"What three times the first day? no, no," said Joseph, laughing, "that would be laying it on too thick."

I came up just then, and found Joseph beset by people as glad to see him as I was.

"Now Joseph," I said, "take my advice, go in for everything; come in the afternoon and come in the evening too, and then I want you to be present at a prayer meeting at my house after the service!"

"Very well, very well," replied Joseph.

He came to all these services and meetings, and had of course to bear the jeers of his companions in the workshop on Monday morning, and certainly, from all accounts, they did not spare him; but he was firm this time, and said he would go to a meeting again that very evening; and there he appeared accordingly.

Several times he attended religious services during that week, and came fearlessly the next Sunday to church, getting quite confirmed in goodness, and he became quite a changed man to all outward appearance, and very well satisfied with himself. His outward life was reformed, but his heart was still unchanged. However, he was *in the way*, and being in the way, the Lord met him.

It so happened that "the Word which is as a hammer," broke the stony heart of one whom he had brought to hear it one day, and he was amazed at the effect of it, for his friend broke down in the presence of the people, and cried aloud for mercy in the greatest trouble of mind. Joseph stood by as one petrified, he saw the agony and distress of this man's soul, and heard his cry, and watched him till the poor man was brought from sorrow and

despair of conviction, to the joy of pardon and peace. No
sooner had the man found peace, than he hurried to
Joseph, and began to exhort him to give his whole heart
to the Lord too.

Joseph went home that evening a convicted man, he
had discovered that his church-going, and his prayers and
good works were not conversion. By degrees he seemed
to wake up from his sleep, and to remember that he had
not been taught and exhorted to mend his life or reform
his own character, but to come to Jesus as a sinner, that
he might be born again and receive forgiveness of sins.
He sought for this and found it, and was found of God,
and then his joy was unbounded.

All in a few weeks the once scornful infidel was converted, and became a joyful christian, and began to enquire in his factory among the several hundreds of men
who worked there, how many of them knew the Lord, and
was astonished to find how few, how very few they were.

This circumstance weighed much on his mind, till one
morning, (he had been praying about it,) while looking
at the hundreds who were pouring out of the various out-
lets of the factory at the breakfast hour, into the court-
yard within the outer gate, he was constrained to cry out,
" What a shame! what a shame! "   He was overcome
and burst into tears, and held up his hands, and cried out
again with a loud voice, " What a shame! " as he stood
with his back to the gate, beside the little wicket through
which the men, one by one, had to pass.

" What's the matter, Joseph?" said several voices,
" what's the matter?"

" What a shame," he replied, " that Christ has so few,
and the devil so many in this factory!   What a shame!"

The men all seemed to feel this cry, it came from the
heart, and went to their hearts.

Joseph used to be a great favourite among his work-
fellows; they knew what he had been, and now they were
struck with the change. The man, who from fear and
from shame could not face his companions once, now was

able to stand before them all, and bear a testimony for God, and plead for men's souls with tears. Joseph's testimony was not in vain; many from that time began to attend the meetings for prayer and praise, heard the gospel and were converted, till the majority of the people in that factory were the Lord's.

A happy day was the Lord's day, and a happy place was the Lord's house, and happy were many who assembled there, and happy was Joseph, who had had the privilege of persuading many to come there. He had been instrumental in watering many souls, and his own soul was watered. Nor did the Lord overlook his family at home; they were all, by the mercy of God, brought to know Him. He believed and he was saved, and his house.

AWAKE, my soul, in joyful lays,
And sing thy great Redeemer's praise;
He justly claims a song from me;
His loving-kindness, oh, how free!

He saw me ruined in the fall,
Yet loved me, notwithstanding all;
He saved me from my lost estate;
His loving-kindness, oh, how great!

Though numerous hosts of mighty foes,
Though earth and hell my way oppose,
He safely leads my soul along;
His loving-kindness, oh, how strong!

Often I feel my sinful heart
Prone from my Saviour to depart;
But, though I have Him oft forgot,
His loving-kindness changes not.

THE SILVER LADDER.

REAMS come sometimes from the thoughts of tne day, sometimes they are suggested by the evil one to lead to sinful words and deeds, and sometimes, we may be sure, they are sent by God to teach or warn us. But how shall we discern and try a dream? By the one test by which we are commanded, "to try the spirits whether they be of God"—that is, by the word. "To the law and to the testimony: if they speak not according to this word, it is because there is no light in them." *Isaiah* viii. 20.

The following dream was told me by the man himself who dreamed it, who has now been a consistent happy christian for fourteen or fifteen years, honouring God in his house, and living a self-denying life to the glory of God. The Lord has indeed blessed him and made him a blessing to a great many, not so much in public speaking, but in what is harder still, in consistent living and personal dealing with souls. He came to me one evening when I had been speaking of the ladder in Jacob's dream. The words he had heard brought to his remembrance very freshly his own vision, and he was stirred up to come and tell it. He said,

"Some years ago, when I was a careless and prayerless young man, I dreamed that I was with nineteen other

men of about my own age in a pleasant place; the house
was good and well furnished with everything we wanted;
the gardens were spacious and delightful, and there was
nothing that we could desire which was not readily and
easily provided for us.

"We all understood that the premises belonged to
Satan, and that he was the master over us, and that he
gave us all these enjoyments freely, upon two conditions:
first, that we were *not to pray*; and secondly, that we were
not to escape from the place. We thought the conditions
were most favourable, for we laughed at the idea of praying; not being of that sort, we were not likely to break
that rule; and as to escaping from the garden, why should
we, when we had all that we could wish for where we
were? It seemed strange to us that our master should
have made no worse conditions."

No, the prince of this world says, even to the child of
God, "All these things will I give thee, and the glory of
them, if thou wilt fall down and worship me;" but where
he gets a willing homage, there is no need to tempt.
Alas! how many there are who have no other lord but
Satan; who desire nothing more for themselves and their
children than the riches, and honours, and pleasures of
this world. They would laugh at the idea of praying,
they are no saints or hypocrites, not given to psalm singing or serious thoughts about death or eternity, and they
have no wish to abandon the world and its gains, not even
at God's command, for they say, if we did not do this and
gain that, others would. No, they have no wish to leave
this world, it is their home, and where should they go?
"No one knows where!" Death is a leap in the dark to
them, and the world is heaven, and indeed all the home
and all the heaven they can ever have, and after that the
judgment. But let us go on with the dream.

"It came to pass after a time, with one and another of
us, that we got *weary* of our pleasures, we were sick and
tired of the place, the dress, the meat, the drink, the
dances, the daily round of gaiety and frivolity did not

satisfy us, and one and all we longed to escape from the place; but how was it to be done? we had pledged ourselves not to pray, and not to escape.

So it is, worldly men are entangled by the laws of society, etiquette, fashion, custom, and though they are sick of their thraldom, yet they remain quite powerless to escape; they cannot pray, to dig they are ashamed; and so they abandon themselves—how many, to recklessness, and float away down the everflowing stream which tends towards the gulf of destruction, tied hand and foot, and ignorant, and callous; what slavery can be more degrading and more cruel than this?

See the poor negroes torn from their homes, chained in gangs, and driven along to the ship, in the stifling hold of which they are to be imprisoned till they land in the *place of slavery*, often unpitying, cruel, heartless slavery. But this is as nothing compared with soul captives; the souls chained in gangs, the never-dying souls which are held in stifling dens of vice and blasphemy, and drunkenness, to be released hereafter only into the *outer darkness* of eternal misery, where shall be weeping and wailing, and gnashing of teeth, and remorse, unavailing bitter remorse, and never-changing anguish! You must not pray, and you must not escape; these are the two conditions. Oh! worldly man, worldly woman, *stop and consider*. Care for yourselves, and care for your children. The prince of this world is not your true master; he has usurped his power, and unlawfully retains it by lying devices; you may escape, you may pray; there is a way of deliverance. Oh, may you find it before it is too late!

"In my dream I saw that our master had provided himself with a great whip. When he observed that we were not enjoying ourselves as usual, he suspected that we were meditating some escape from his influence and power, and he threatened us loudly,

"'Hark ye, you slaves! if you dare to pray, or if you dare to escape, I'll have you!'

"We trembled at him, and no longer laughed at the

idea of praying, or escaping either. How I longed to begin—but he seemed to know it, for one day he coaxed me to pleasure, and because I would not, he stung me with his whip.

"'Taste that! and that is what you shall have; you are the most disaffected of all.'

"After a time, others came under that cruel and withering lash; we were in despair, and our master walked about on the watch, day and night, to prevent our praying and escaping; we were not permitted to speak to one another lest we should conspire against him. Now was our case most miserable, and we knew not which way to turn. We contrived however to make it known among ourselves, that at a certain time, as many of us as were so disposed should pray, one in one place and one in another, so that at least a few might escape, while the others were being scourged. We seemed instinctively to know that prayer was our only way of effectual escape. Some had prayed, and been punished till they desisted, and some had endeavoured to flee, but had been captured and brought back to heavier bondage.

"On the set day and time, my place was behind some bales, unopened bales of costly goods—costly, but quite useless to us; we had no pleasure in them. In this dark corner I knelt down and quickly began to pray to God to forgive and deliver me. But soon I heard the master's whip and his blasphemous voice; his fury was terrible, but I prayed all the more intensely, when I heard his footsteps approaching me.

"'Aha! you are there, are you?'

"And then he cracked his whip, till my heart trembled within me. I opened my eyes, and behold, in the dark corner, there was a beautiful silver ladder all ready. How long it had been there I know not, but it was the work of an instant to leap into it, and with hands and feet to climb for my life.

"'I'll teach you to climb,' said the master, and calmly began to ascend too.

"My terror was very great when I felt the ladder shaking under me. I almost let go my hold for fear, for his cool determination to destroy me, and the slow words of wrath which he spoke, almost unnerved me, and I looked up to see how much further I had to go; and I saw that at the head of the silver ladder, even if I could reach it, there was only a *very small* aperture, scarcely large enough for one hand. My master seemed to see the look I gave, and appeared to know my thoughts.

"'You cannot escape—I'll have you—and you will never, never climb again!' he said.

"But with a fresh gush of energy I made a new start to climb, and my master simultaneously came striding up, and I felt his hot sulphury breath on the back of my neck, while he thundered awful oaths in my ear; but I climbed on for sweet life, and came to the hole and thrust my hand through, and then my arm, and then my head, and then my other arm. And now the struggle for life!—and I know not how it was, but I was safe on the other side, and my late master was raging furiously below.

"I stopped to breathe a little, I know not how long, I was in such a state of excitement, and then when I came to myself, there were beautiful fields of living green around me, and glorious flowers, and angels flying about like birds. Some of them came to welcome me, and they rejoiced over me, and I said, 'Where is the Lord of this beautiful place?' There He was before me, standing with His hand stretched out: I saw the fresh wound in His white hand, and I bowed down before Him, and could not thank Him enough for joy. He bade me rise, but still I continued prostrate, and He said,

"'What is thy petition?'

"I said, 'Oh! my Lord, there are nineteen more down there'—and I shuddered at the remembrance—'I pray Thee, make that hole larger;' but He, with the sweetest smile, said,

"'It is large enough for each one—I have made it so—fear not;' and then I awoke."

"Tell me," said I, when he had finished the story of the dream, "tell me what did you do when you awoke?"

He said he could do nothing, his heart was throbbing and beating so, that another person might have heard the sound of it.

"Did you not get up and pray?"

"No, I was afraid."

He said, for days and days he felt so miserable, he was tempted to destroy himself; when he knelt to pray he was afraid of being seen, and he could not keep his mind to his prayer for watching, lest some one should catch him praying. One day, some of his fellow-workmen were laughing at men who prayed, and one turned to him and said,

"There's Thomas, he looks full of shame; I should not wonder if he turns out one of these praying hypocrites."

"Whenever I knelt or tried to pray, such evil, cursed thoughts came into my mind—such filthy thoughts and oaths sometimes, that I could not pray. I felt very like myself in the old master's premises again."

"One Sunday I was passing by a cottage in a country lane, and I heard a man's voice say, clearly,

'Jesus, the Name high over all, in hell, or earth, or sky—
  Angels and men before it fall, and devils fear and fly.'

I listened, and presently voices sang that verse; I had never, I thought, heard such singing; men, women, and children seemed to be singing, and I was not, and sorrow filled my heart. Presently they stopped, and again the voice I had heard before gave out another verse:

'Jesus the pris'ners' fetters breaks, and bruises Satan's head;
  Power into strengthless souls He speaks, and life into the dead.

I felt a love for those people, and a love for the Jesus of whom they were singing.

'O that the world might taste and see the riches of His grace;
  The arms of love that compass me, would all mankind embrace.'

After they had sung this, and repeated the last two lines fervently, a man began to pray; his prayer was, as it were, all about me. I was melted to the earth, and cannot tell how I felt till some one stood by me and kindly bade me come in. Oh, how kind were these strangers to me! they prayed for me, they cheered and bid me pray too, but I could not get on; it seemed all clear and easy to them, but not so with me. They would not let me go till I promised to come again in the evening. I did so, and there the Lord opened my eyes to see the way of salvation, and then I saw how the Lamb of God had borne my sins and made atonement to God; the burden rolled off my soul, and I praised the Lord heartily. Oh! how happy were these people at my release. They said the angels were rejoicing over me in heaven. I am sure they were like the angels, they were rejoicing on earth. Since that I have served the Lord, and I wish I could serve Him more fully."

I have often heard from my friend, of the love and blessing of God to him, and how he is used of God to win souls for Jesus.

RICHARD'S VICTORY.

HAT a solemn, yet joyful place is that where a blood-washed soul is departing.

> "When angels are from glory come,
> Are round the bed and in the room,
> Waiting to take the Spirit home."

Sorrowing relatives and weeping sisters stood near, and Richard said,

"How can you cry for me? I am going to glory; this is glory—this is heaven—this is victory—don't weep for me."

> "Come sing to me of heaven,
> When I'm about to die;
> Sing songs of holy ecstacy
> To wait my soul on high."

> "There will be no more sorrow there,
> In heaven above, where all is love,
> There will be no more sorrow there."

"If ever I loved Thee, my Jesus, 'tis now," and thus Richard departed, who, only a few months before, had been living without hope and without God in the world, a Christless soul.

I do not tell this to recommend a death-bed conversion, or to commend a life spent unprofitably in sins, but to shew the wonderful pardoning love of God, and the manifest change He can work by His Holy Spirit upon ordinary men.

When I first saw Richard it was autumn, and the chill of winter was creeping on, the leaves were sear and falling, the lane was thickly strewed with them, he was slowly and feebly walking along under the shelter of a hedge. He had been a strong, brave man, but now his constitution was undermined by consumption, and he was failing in strength and breath, and sinking into the grave.

Seeing that he looked dejected and cheerless, I was moved to speak to him kindly, but he seemed quite indifferent to my words, and was absorbed in his own ailments. I asked where he lived, and promised to call and see him, but he did not encourage me in that either, or manifest any desire for it. However, as I had promised I went and sat with him, and read to him, and spoke of his danger, shewing him that his fleeting breath was all that now detained him from a sinner's final doom, and that his danger was all the greater and more serious because he did not feel it.

I proved the reality of these things from the word of God, and assured him that the same Holy Spirit who had written this description of the sinner's state and danger, had done so on purpose to make us value so much the more the wonderful salvation, which God had provided for us in Christ Jesus.

He was attending to me as he afterwards assured me, but at the time he did not seem sufficiently interested to encourage me very much. I prayed with him, and was led, in spite of discouragements to promise him another visit, though he never thanked me for this one, or invited another. I was taken to him again not long after, without having any desire or design to go, and again I spoke to him of the great salvation, that it was *full, free, and present—a present salvation*. How shall we escape if we neglect it? and still he seemed unmoved and listless.

After this I yet paid him five or six visits, during which time I saw he was rapidly sinking and failing in strength, till at length he was confined to his house. Unable to get out, he used to creep down from his bed to the fireside, and then in the evening make his weary way back to his sleepless bed again, where he suffered for hours and hours, coughing and tossing about in pain and restlessness, without any comforting or hopeful thoughts to cheer him.

It was enough to bring him to submission, but yet, though he was sometimes conscious that his life was ebbing away, he seemed quite unmoved.

One day I was led to say to him, "I don't see the use of coming all this way to you so often, particularly as you don't seem to care for my visits, and don't do as I tell you. I think I had better leave you, for a time at least, so I will read a little and then go, for I might just as well stay at home and talk to my mantel-piece as talk to you!"

Accordingly after prayer, I was about to depart, when he said, looking up at me in a most despairing way,

"Don't leave me;" it seemed to make amends for all his past silence.

"But," said I, "what is the good?"

"Oh, yes, there is good," he replied; "I remember all you have said, and I have tried to do it. I know what you say is all true, and I know how bad I am; I know I'm a sinner—I'm a lost sinner; I shall be damned for ever if I die as I am, I know that."

This was a long speech for this man to make, so I sat down again, and began to make up his little fire for him, while he became calm and regained his breath, and also I was seeking guidance.

"Why do you not give yourself up to the Lord," I enquired, "and pray to Him?"

"I do," he answered, looking at a particular chair as if that could testify to the truth and reality of his effort; "I do, but when I kneel down, such blasphemous and wicked thoughts come to my mind, and all kinds of worldly things, so that I am obliged to give it all up; I cannot pray. I cannot help thinking God is unkind to me, and so harsh, that I feel more inclined to swear than to pray. I have tried very hard, I cannot pray, I must give it up."

My heart was drawn to this poor tempted one, I said,
"*Do not give up, whatever you do.* I am not discouraged
if you are; no, to tell the truth, it is rather a good sign that
Satan thinks it worth his while to trouble you like this."

He looked surprised at me.

"Do not suppose," I continued, "that God would
invite you to pray and then hinder you. To be sure not.
It is Satan; he sees that you are really in earnest, and
that you are likely to escape from him, so he tries to hinder you. Look at it in the true light, and you will see
that Satan's opposition is not a bad sign; when you were
living without prayer and really displeasing God, he did
not discourage you then, did he? Now take my advice,
the Scripture tells us to 'resist the devil,' and promises
'he shall flee,' for God will drive him away. The next
time you are tempted, don't get up from your knees,
but ask God to help you to resist the temptation; you are
sure to prevail.

"John Bunyan used to be dreadfully tempted in the
same way, when he was seeking God, and he knew that
the doubts which harassed him were from the devil.
'While I was at prayer,' he says, 'I uttered words to this
effect: O Lord, Satan tells me that neither Thy mercy
nor Christ's blood is sufficient to save my soul; Lord,
shall I honour *Thee* most by believing that Thou wilt or
canst save me, or *him* by believing that Thou neither wilt
nor canst?' He soon had his answer, and you know what
a valiant Christian John Bunyan afterwards became.
Do not be discouraged, cheer up and have your battle
out, and you shall have a *victory* too, I have no doubt
about it."

So saying I rose to go, promising to return again very
soon and to hear all about it. He begged me not to go,
but I thought it better to leave him for the present alone
with God.

In the evening, before his bed-time, I called to see him
again and to hear how he had sped, and found him, as I
expected, wonderfully changed and softened, as if he had

seen the hand of the Lord. The dear man was quite melted with a sense of God's kindness, and with sorrow for having distrusted Him. I said,

"He is a very present help in trouble, is He not? God is love, and He loves you, that is very clear. He gave His Son to die instead of you, do you believe it? if you do, thank Him for His love, and trust Him through everything."

He replied saying something, as people usually do, about "not feeling," but I had not asked him to thank God for feelings, but rather for Christ's manifested love in dying for him. Thank Him for dying for you; thank Him for His love.

> "A guilty, weak, and helpless worm,
>   On Thy kind arms I fall;
> Be Thou my Strength and Righteousness,
>   My Jesus, and my all."

He begged me to say this again, and ejaculated as I repeated the verse, "That's it, yes, that's true; say it again: 'Be Thou my Jesus, *my* Saviour, *my* all!'"

His soul was being quickened with Divine power, and the fire was beginning to burn in his heart, kindling up his countenance with new joy and thankfulness, till at last he burst out in praises, giving God hearty thanks for his deliverance.

Now he was saved and happy; and what a manifest change was there in that man. He could not rest that night for joy, and gladly he testified to his relatives, telling them what the Lord had done for his soul. The neighbours came to see him and wondered, for they could scarcely believe their eyes and ears when they saw the change which had been wrought. The dumb spirit was gone, and he could talk now quite freely about the love of God. That one who used to be so sad and lonely and silent, now was bright and cheerful, and always in happy company; and, though his weakness was increasing and his life was visibly ebbing away, he did not heed it, for he seemed to forget himself and his bodily state altogether, in the gladness and rejoicing which filled his soul.

He spoke and lived like one beside himself, and so he was, for he was out of himself, a new man; and the Lord had given him a new heart and put a new spirit within him.

Reader, I will not ask you what you *think* about this, but I would affectionately ask, do you know in your own experience about it? Have you gained a victory yet through the blood of the Lamb? This is, it is true, but the beginning of victories, just only as it were the alphabet of Christ's religion, yet it is most important and necessary as an entrance into the christian warfare. You must conquer or be conquered; you must be changed before you die or perish for ever. It is not necessary for every one to be brought to the Lord precisely in the same way, and with the same experience, but everyone who has been quickened and converted knows and understands that once he was dead in trespasses and sins, and that now by grace he is made alive; and he can understand also, and know what has taken place in others who have received the same gift of grace, and can sympathize and rejoice with them.

Richard lived for several months testifying with great joy before the final scenes transpired which have been described in the beginning of the tract; and his testimony was blessed to the conversion of some of his neighbours and relations, who are doing now in their health and strength what he never did—*living to serve the Lord,* which is far better than a death-bed conversion.

I LOVE Thee, because Thou hast first loved me,
  And purchased my pardon on Calvary's tree;
I love Thee, for wearing the thorns on Thy brow;
If ever I loved Thee, my Jesus, 'tis now.

I'll love Thee in life, *and I'll love Thee in death,*
And praise Thee as long as Thou lendest me breath;
And say, when the death-dew lies cold on my brow,
If ever I loved Thee, my Jesus, 'tis now.

IN MANSIONS OF GLORY, AND ENDLESS DELIGHT,
I'LL EVER ADORE THEE IN YON HEAVEN OF LIGHT;
I'll sing with the glittering crown on my brow,
IF EVER I LOVED THEE, MY JESUS, 'TIS NOW.

NOT A WALL, BUT A DOOR.

><

OUR good Lord, who loveth not the death of a
sinner, but rather that he should turn and live,
has opened a door for us as a way of access to
Himself. To confirm the truth of His words of
invitation, He has given us many undeserved proofs of
the reality of His kind intention.

A woman called me into her cottage one morning as I
was passing by, and told me of her son, a steady young
man, though still unconverted, for whom she had prayed
continually, ever since his birth. She said, when he was
a very little child, she heard him one night sobbing and
praying in his room—"O Lord, save me up for a good
boy!" She thought this was in answer to her supplication; but as he grew up he became thoughtless and
careless, like too many others of his age.

Some five or six months ago, she said, "He had a dream
or vision, and saw you so plainly that he pointed you
out to me, among other clergymen, and said, 'Mother,
that man is to be our minister one day. I saw him a
little time ago, in a dream, as plainly as I see him now;
I know that is the man.' We did not know who you
were then, or where you came from, and never saw you
again till you came lately to this parish to be our minister.

"Last night," continued the mother, "after he returned
from church, my William was very unhappy and restless;

and in the night I heard him crying and praying aloud
for mercy, in great distress. He told me this morning
when I asked him about it, that he dreamed that the last
day was come, and that the world was on fire; and he
began immediately to try to pray, but he could not; yet
he went on trying till he heard some one laugh out at
him, and say, 'Ho! ho! my boy, you are too late!—ho!
ho!—too late! I have got you now—you are too late!'
This frightened him so much that he woke up, and getting out of bed, began to pray on his knees in earnest for
the Lord to have mercy on his soul."

Being much interested in the young man, I begged her
to send him to me in the evening. She did so, and we
may well understand that it was not long before the
Lord, who had so marvellously opened his eyes to see his
sins, enabled him by the same Spirit to see Jesus as his
Saviour, and to rejoice in the forgiveness of his sins.

When he arrived I frankly told him what I had heard
about him, and particularly about his distress and prayer
the night before.

"Your mother has prayed for you for years, and when
you were a little boy you prayed the Lord to save you;
and last night again you were constrained to cry for
mercy. These are all tokens of God's good intentions
and purposes towards you. Can you trust Him?"

As he hesitated, for so many like to feel something
before they make the venture of faith, I continued,

"These tokens are better than feelings, for they are
facts, and sure signs by which you may assuredly know
that the Lord is calling you."

After we had prayed together I asked him to sit down
again, for I had a question to ask him. I was curious to
hear about the dream or vision which he had had some
months before he ever saw me.

"William," said I, "did you ever see me before I came
to this parish?"

"Yes," he replied, "I saw you once in a vision more
than six months ago!"

"Do you mind telling me about it?"

After a little hesitation he answered, "I often dream things. One night I dreamed that I was walking on a wild barren common; there were many bare places where people had cut turf, and there were prickly furze bushes about, and I knew there were some old open mine-shafts there, for people sometimes fell into them in the night; but I was walking along without thinking of danger, and I was not afraid though it was dark and I was alone. I don't know how long I went on like this, but next I found I was walking with you. I could see you very plainly, just as if it had not been dark, and you were talking about Jesus and His love to sinners. I liked your words very much, and was so taken up with them that I do not know when it became quite light, for now I could see the rough common, and after a little I saw there was a path, and we were walking in it. Going along this path we came to a wall, and I could not go any further; but you walked on as if there were no wall. Presently, you stopped and turned to me, and said,

"'Why don't you come on?'

"I answered, 'I cannot.'

"'Why not?'

"'Because there is a wall here!'

"'No,' you said, 'there is no wall, it is an open door.'

"I was surprised at your saying that, for I could feel the wall and see it, and yet you went through and were standing before me.

"'Not a wall, but a door,' you said; 'walk on, forward!'

"When I ventured forward I found your words were true, and it was indeed an open way, and it led into a beautiful garden. I was very happy, and said, 'Whose garden is this?'

"You answered, 'It is the Lord's garden, and you are to dress it and keep it and work in it.'

"Then I saw the Lord Himself—He came forward and

kindly bid me welcome, and said that you should teach
me for three years, and then I woke."

"Can you see the meaning of your dream?" I asked.

"Oh, yes," said William; "I wonder I did not think
of it before."

How many are walking in danger of those deep shafts
in bare places and thorny ways, wandering about in the
dark?

The first time William heard me preach he saw the
way open before him, but still, somehow, he could not go
in; he seemed to be waiting for some obstacles to be removed, or some openings to be made, or some work of the
Spirit to be done, before he could dare to venture in.
The finished work of Christ on the cross is as an open
door that the Lord has set before perishing sinners, that
they may escape from danger and get peace and salvation;
but instead of availing themselves of it, they stop and
hesitate and doubt, till they feel as if there were a high
wall and barrier before them which they could not pass.

Sinner, His love unknown has broken every barrier
down. Do you know that? Have you proved it? Are
you forgiven? You may indeed come to Him *just as you
are*, without any other plea but that His blood has been
shed for you, and His word has bidden you; why then
should you tarry? "Oh, there is a wall here," you cry;
"an impossibility. I cannot! I cannot!"

You are bidden and commanded to come *now;* and the
Lord who thus bids you, knows you, and all about your
state and your sins and sinfulness far better than you do.
If He bids you come *now*, it must be *just as you are;* and
there must be an open door of access, the same through
which He speaks to you, by the same you may come.

Some plead the Lord's dignity and majesty, as King
of kings and Lord of lords, and that He may not be
approached without a human, though divinely-commis-
sioned mediator. I love those who really exalt the honour
and majesty of God. But this plea is not a wall. There
is a Mediator, the Lord Jesus Himself; and He is *the*

door; He says it of Himself. "I am (not *a*, but) *the* Door; by Me, if any man enter in, he shall be saved." *St. John* x. 9. "If any man,"—what can be more open than this?

Some plead, in feelings of sincerity, their utter unworthiness of any such kindness and mercy; they have sinned, yea, even against light, and love, and mercy, willingly and wilfully. This is not a wall either, but just the very confession which can touch the compassionate heart of Jesus, who knows how sorely we are let and hindered from within and without. He loves to set the captive free. He has need of such to exercise His office upon, and to do His loving work of deliverance.

Some plead their helplessness; they have the will and desire, but no power; they cannot pray; they cannot believe—they cannot feel; it is a dead, cold, hard obstacle that stands in their path; but even this is not a wall. What better prayer can there be than that of helplessness? What more effectual cry to One who loves to grant, than that of the sinking soul which cries "I cannot pray, I cannot believe; oh, help mine unbelief!" This has proved a very door of liberty to many souls.

Some plead their want of will and desire; they understand and know and in their conscience feel that they ought to yield themselves to God, but there is no inclination in that direction, for all their heart's desires are for the world and its pleasures; their heart is warm towards this world and cold towards God—dead as a stone, and unfeeling about heavenly things. But even this need not be a barrier, for who can subdue the unruly will or sinful affection but the Lord? Who can take away the heart of stone and give a feeling heart of flesh but the Lord? Oh reader, whatever be your state or your case, it is not too hard for the Almighty God. Is there any thing too hard for Him? Would He not cease to be *Almighty*, if there were, and would not His highest and greatest prerogative of mercy be hindered? He loves to shew His almighty power most chiefly in shewing mercy and pity; only venture on Him, and prove Him, and you will see for yourself how much more ready He is to give than you to ask.

So that whether you be one who trembles to come before God without a mediator; or whether you feel your utter sinfulness and unworthiness; or your helplessness; or you are conscious of *unwillingness;* yet there is a Mediator, thank God, and He has all-prevailing merit, and is strong to save and deliver you. The very excuses and hindrances which seem to bid us stop, are in fact the very causes and reasons for going forward. What seems a wall to us, is in very truth a door of liberty, which God has opened to us, through the prevailing merit of Jesus. The stopping places of nature are the starting places of grace.

"Come and see," said Jesus. Come and see for yourself—taste and see how gracious the Lord is! The door is open! Truly blessed is the man that trusteth in Him.

> "I heard the voice of Jesus say,
>   Come unto me and rest;
> Lay down, thou weary one, lay down,
>   Thy head upon my breast.
> I came to Jesus as I was,
>   Weary, and worn, and sad;
> I found in Him a resting place,
>   And He has made me glad."

"I came to Jesus as I was"—this just makes all the difference between the man who has salvation, and the man who has not. William, in his dream, simply acted on the word which was given to him, though, as he said, he felt he had a wall before him. He stepped out nevertheless, as if there was not a wall but a door, and he found it was so. Indeed, it proved to him to be the door to privileges for which he had long been waiting. He entered in, and has ever since been holding on his way, working out his own salvation, making it like a garden of the Lord, fragrant and profitable, God working in him to will and to do of His good pleasure. He had the help he was promised for just three years, and since that, he has been instrumental in blessing to many souls, and encouraging many by his example, and exhorting many by his words. The Lord did not forget the prayer he offered in his early childhood, or overlook his mother's continued supplications on his behalf.

May this story encourage many parents to pray with expectation and confidence; and teach many faint-hearted ones to refuse to stand any longer outside an open door. May they be strengthened to venture in boldly, since it is God who bids them; and the all-powerful and meritorious blood of Jesus, which was shed for all, has paid the price for their admission and welcome.

THE LORD'S MESSENGER.

"WHAT went ye out for to see?" asked the Lord Jesus of the multitude who had heard John the Baptist's question: "Art thou He that should come, or shall we look for another?"

The Lord exalted His faithful and good servant in the eyes of the people, at a time when he was to outward appearance, at least, as one cast aside, and given over into the hands of his enemies, and imprisoned.

What went ye out to see on Jordan's banks when John was preaching with superhuman power, thrilling the hearts of his hearers, and awakening their consciences?— A reed shaken with the wind?—A poor weak thing swayed about, and blown to and fro by the unseen breeze? No! this was one who was filled with the Spirit; his very soul was full, and out of the overflowing abundance of his heart he spoke, not swayed from without, but constrained from within, words of God and words of conscious power.

But what went ye out to see, a man clothed in soft raiment? such are in kings' houses. This rugged man of stern truths, and unwelcome and rough tidings, was in the bare wilderness.

But what went ye out to see, a prophet? Yea, he was more than a prophet; he not only cried Repent! but beyond others who predicted the coming Messiah, he was able to "behold the Lamb of God," and to point Him

out. This is he, the man filled with the abiding Spirit of
God, speaking faithful words to God-hating, sin-stricken
mortals, the man who can see and shew Jesus. This is
He of whom it is written, Behold, I send *my messenger
before thy face to prepare thy way before thee.*

John the Baptist was the harbinger of Christ, and so
are Christians, likewise, in one sense, God the Father's
messengers, sent by Him to prepare the way for Christ
to come to the hearts of others, who in their turn should
become messengers also. But how often is this high
honour and privilege of being God's messenger forgotten
or overlooked by Christians!

No doubt charity begins at home, and our first work is
in our ownselves, and we need to prepare the way of
Christ in our own hearts, and to be filled with the Holy
Spirit, and to keep ourselves in subjection to God, and to
be followers of Jesus; but this is not all our work here
below. He has promised, "ye also shall bear witness of
me." *John* xv. 27. It changes the self-denying character of Christ's religion into a kind of selfishness, when we
are seeking only our own sanctification, and much more
so when we are seeking only our own salvation. But
how often, I say, do people overlook this purpose of
their conversion, and the joys and privileges of it!

A young lady who had been arrested in the midst of
her worldliness and levity, by the alarming illness of her
mother, and then awakened and brought to Jesus by her
faithful and true words, went on her way rejoicing, in the
assured forgiveness of her sins, but she had never heard
that she was expected to bear a testimony for Jesus, and
shew forth His praise by recommending Him as a Saviour
to others.

One day she was impressed by the thoughts with
which we have begun our tract, and being anxious to
know more on the subject, she was not afraid or ashamed
(as too many are) to learn about it, so she spoke to the
friend who had brought the subject before her.

"What do you think you were converted for?"

She answered, "To be saved."

"What were you saved for? But let me put another question: What were you saved from?"

Her countenance brightened with joy and thankfulness at this, and she replied, "He saved me; 'He brought me up also out of an horrible pit, out of the miry clay, and set my feet upon a rock, and established my goings; and He hath put a new song in my mouth, even praise unto our God.'"

"Thank God," said the responsive heart to which she spoke. "The Lord's people ever speak from heart to heart, as their Heavenly Father speaks to them. Thank God, but pray go on with your quotation. So turning to the 40th Psalm, she read, "Many shall see it and fear, and shall trust in the Lord."

"'Many *shall see it;*'" see what? Your testimony of Jesus and salvation. How did you, and how can so many overlook this? Were you really saved from the pit, was it indeed horrible, most horribly dark and full of despair, and would you have perished for ever if you had died in that pit? Where you were by nature, *all others are*, whether they be religious or irreligious, moral or immoral, till they have been taken out! My child, did you ever tell your widowed father what the Lord had done for your soul?"

"No, he would laugh at me; my dying mother's words had no effect on him."

"But, my child, have you ever considered what must become of your father if he should die as he is? and having felt the danger of the pit yourself, can you not feel for the danger of those dear to you, and all the more because they do not feel it themselves?"

With real trouble she said, "Oh, I cannot bear to think of it."

"Yes, but is it not most selfish of you to let people go unwarned, because you cannot bear to think of their danger; how will they bear it, when they are irrecoverably engulfed, and how will you reflect on yourself, when they are gone beyond your reach?"

"Oh, but I cannot speak to papa; oh, no, indeed I could not."

"My dear child, will you ask God to speak through you, and you be as all Christians should be, only *the voice of one* speaking, would you not rejoice to be God's messenger to your father for the good of his soul? Could you not tell him what were your dear mother's words to you, how they impressed you, and what effect they produced on you? Often and often your mother prayed for him, as well as for you; her prayers are partly answered, and you saved, and how do you know but that the remainder of the answer is kept back on purpose to give you the privilege of being instrumental in God's hand, in procuring it?"

The thought charmed her, and she immediately begged, "Oh, pray for me."

Accordingly we knelt down and prayed to the Lord, and she rose from her knees full of zeal; but alas, it was not so easy to begin now, as it would have been if she had spoken out in the first outburst of her overflowing heart. Nevertheless her prayer was before the Lord, and the more she prayed, the more her love for her father and his best interests engrossed her thoughts, and out of the fulness of her heart she often endeavoured to speak, but something ever hindered her. Sometimes when she was alone with him she though she would, but her tongue cleaved to the roof of her mouth! She choked with emotion and was dumb, and though she was not aware of it, the struggle did not escape her father's observing eye; and he wondered what could be the matter with his much-loved motherless child.

One day when she had prayed more than usual for help, and begged that some opening might be given for speaking, her father came into the room and said to her,

"What is the matter with you, my child? are you anxious about anything?"

Her poor heart throbbed now with her emotion.

"What is it, my child, are you ill? are you unhappy about anything? About my health? Tell me!"

"Yes, papa," but she could utter no more; he caressed her, and bade her not fear, for he was much better than he had been; she would not be quite an orphan yet, and even "if it should so please the Almighty, I have made good provision for you."

He then left her, hastily to hide his own emotion, having very little suspicion as to the real cause of her misery. The dumb spirit possessed her and she could not speak, but she could still pray, and pray on she did, till at last, one evening when she could not rest any longer, armed with fresh courage and zeal, she came to her father and began to speak to him. The conversation between them very soon verged on the point near her heart, and then agitation and dumbness again possessed her, till at last, to her disappointment, it came to bed time, and so another day was gone!

She fled to her room in distress, and besought the Lord to help her, and then—for where there is a will there is ever a way also—then she sat down and wrote a short note to her father. How much may be said *in a few words*, when the things we would say have been well steeped in a heart of prayer, whereas how little is said in many words under other circumstances. She wrote her note, and tapping at her father's door, slipped it under the door to him and retreated to her own chamber, and there again on her knees, begged the Lord to bless the words.

While she was thus engaged, her father was reading the note she had given him, and at length apprehending her meaning, and just blinded with his tears, he cried, "Ah! I see it all now! That dear child is anxious *for my soul*," and he was quite overcome.

Taking the note in his hand, he went across to her room, and finding her on her knees, he knelt by her side, and said, "My loving child, pray for your old sinful father," and the poor man trembled and sobbed aloud, completely broken down.

She did pray, and he responded to her prayer and prayed for himself, and the Lord heard and answered that united supplication. The old man's heart was broken, his long stifled convictions now burst on him with new power, for in the midst of all the seeming carelessness and indifference of his manner, he had yet been the subject of very searching thoughts. The Holy Spirit had been working in him, his wife's prayers and words had not been in vain, and now before the throne of grace he sought his pardon from God, who alone can give it, for Jesus' sake, and never rested till he found that pardon and peace which Jesus loves to bestow.

Now, who shall describe the joy of the trembling daughter, her thankfulness to the Lord and her praise!

"We shall see thy dear mother again, my child; we shall be together again! We shall never be parted!"

"Yes, dear father; and let us, before we are called away from this world, be as dear mother was, each of us a messenger *for God*, a messenger of God to *speak of Christ*, of Jesus only."

Art thou content, hast thou no higher aim
　Than just to gain admittance at the door,
In faintest characters to trace thy name
　Among the list of those who die no more?

Dost thou not feel that thou art saved *to live?*
　Dost thou not know that thou art saved *to save?*
Forgiven that thou mightest too forgive,
　Redeemed alike for both sides of the grave?

Saved from the wreck, reach out a saving hand,
　Thousands are sinking 'neath the waves of sin;
Stay not thine efforts till God bids thee land,
　Thy task accomplished, He will steer thee in.

JESUS! and shall it ever be,
    A mortal man ashamed of Thee?
Ashamed of Thee, whom angels praise,
Whose glories shine through endless days?

Ashamed of Jesus! that dear Friend
On whom my hopes of heaven depend!
No; when I blush, be this my shame,
That I no more revere His name.

Till then—nor is my boasting vain—
Till then I boast a Saviour slain;
And, oh, may this my glory be,
That Christ is not ashamed of me!

THE "SECOND LOOK."

SOME people think it is great presumption to speak of the Lord's work in the soul, or to tell of sins forgiven, and the soul saved by that loving Saviour who came to this world on purpose to save sinners, and has "power on earth to forgive sins."

A person in position and authority once quoted this text: "Talk no more so exceeding proudly; let not arrogancy come out of your mouth." 1 *Sam.* ii. 3. And seriously he thought it referred to those who spoke out of the abundance of their hearts of the Lord's goodness to them. One short look at the context would have convinced him how entirely, in every sense, he had mistaken the words; and if he had a conscience at all awakened, he would have felt that they were spoken of such as he was himself. Some people do not like others to speak of experiences which they have not had, though I have known such persons most forward to speak *afterwards*, when they had anything to tell.

It is good to tell of the Lord, and to make our boast, not of ourselves and our attainment, but of Him and His bountiful goodness; and it is good to act promptly on the drawings of the Spirit, and in the way that He draws. The Psalmist says, "When Thou saidst unto me, Seek ye my face, my heart said unto Thee, Thy face, Lord, will I seek." To exemplify or illustrate this, I will tell a story of one who had received a message to his soul, but keeping it to himself, he derived no benefit, whereas telling it was the means of bringing deliverance to his soul.

I went, some years ago, to see a man whom I had observed as a constant and interested hearer at my church. There was something, whether in his expression or manner I know not, which seemed to draw me to him and hold me as with a spell, though I did not know anything about him, and I desired to make his acquaintance. Accordingly I enquired, ascertained where he lived, and went out to find him.

When I had sat down at his bidding and told him I had seen him at church, he suddenly said,

"Oh, I know what you are come for, I will get you my contribution to the Indian mutiny fund."

Before I could reply he was gone, and soon he returned with money in his hand, which he gave me.

"I will deliver this," I said, "to the collectors, but this is not what I came for. I came to speak to you about your soul."

"Oh," said he, "I was at church last night with my friend," naming a person whom I did not know, "he and I wished to speak to you after the service, but we could not make up our minds to go to the vestry, and while we were considering, you opened the door, and we ran away. We came home here and prayed that you might be sent to us."

"Here I am, then," I replied; "surely the Lord has brought me here in answer to your prayer. What can I say to you or do for you?"

He told me he had known better days, but by yielding to temptation and evil companions, he had been led away into bad and drinking habits, and into debt, and had been sent away from his home and country to earn his living in a lower station of life. Now he was married, and was inclined to be steady; but he found it so difficult to become so, and so hard to keep his resolutions. He had taken the pledge several times, but could not keep it.

The last time he fell, he was very firm in refusing to
drink beer and spirits; but while his companion was
drinking wine, he thought within himself, I did not take
any pledge about wine; so he ordered some, and was
soon as bad as ever.

"Do you ever ask God in prayer to help you?"

"Oh yes!"

"Did you ever ask Him to give you a new heart and
to put a new spirit in you, for Jesus' sake?"

"That is just what I wanted to speak to you about last
night," he said; "James and I both agreed that we
would come to you, but we had not courage."

How the Lord marks the efforts of those who are willing, however weak they may be, or however ignorantly
they may be acting. These men had determined to come
and say, "What must we do to be saved?" And though
it may be through their past self-will and self-indulgence
they had so weakened themselves that they could not do
what they would, yet in a way they knew not, they were
helped. They *prayed*, and behold the answer.

In the course of conversation it came out that my
friend's first impressions were made some years ago, before
he fell into the ways of outward sin and immorality we
have mentioned, by a dream or vision of Jesus on the
cross, which had made such an impression on his mind
that he felt it ever since, that the Saviour could and would
deliver him somehow. He was encouraged and cheered
by this prospect sometimes, and sometimes he was led
away in spite of himself into temptation and sin, till he
was filled with despair.

He said, "I saw a figure of Christ on the cross, as large
as life; at first I was going to pass it, but presently I
turned and looked at it attentively, and to my surprise I
saw that the eyes of the figure were open and looking at
me, and then I perceived that the hands and feet were
bleeding. I went on to get a little nearer, but as I went
I stumbled and fell. I got up again in order to go forward, and, looking up, I saw that the figure was come

down from the cross, and was standing on the ground and beckoning to me. A sudden fear came over me, and I stopped. While I was still looking, the vision faded away. But I seem to feel that Jesus is the friend I want, and nothing else and no one else can satisfy me or do me good."

"'Oh that I knew where I could find Him,' is your text," I replied, "and a very good one it is too. You are right in saying no one else can satisfy you, but unfortunately, too many stop instead of going on at the critical point of their history; and sometimes the crisis is not kept on for them as it has been for you till now. It may be you are the child of many prayers. When any one hears the voice of Jesus say 'come;' that is, when the desire is kindled anyhow in your heart, you should come at once, and never rest till you can say, and do say it, 'I came to Jesus as I was.' Jesus only can pardon you, and He has promised, and even *offered* to do it. What a foolish and unthinking thing it is to flee from Him or to fear to go to Him. Long ago there was a sinner arrested in his mad career by a vision similar to yours—he says:

'I saw One hanging on a tree,
    In agony and blood,
Who fixed His languid eyes on me,
    As near His cross I stood.'

"The new object was only an old familiar one, but newly applied to his heart and his *conscience;* he saw it, and observed that its eyes were looking at him. Now mark what was the effect of this—he says:

'It seemed to charge me with His death,
    Though not a word He spoke.'

Here is a true picture of a soul awakened, and under conviction wrought by the Spirit of God. His conscience felt it, and indeed no one could help feeling it; but what I wish to warn you against is, letting the conviction pass away. Remember, the deepest impressions may and do fade away, if you do not *own* or *acknowledge* them. *He owned his guilt*—he owned that he was verily guilty, and that his sins had spilt that blood. Now comes the joyful part of the story; he says:

> 'A *second look* He gave, which said,
> I freely all forgive;
> This blood is for thy ransom paid,
> I die, that you may live.'

"The second look is as much and as clearly a matter of experience as the first; and it comes, you see, after you own your guilt. 'If we confess our sins, God is faithful and just to forgive us our sins, and to cleanse us from all unrighteousness.' Surely if a person knows he is a sinner, he ought not to rest till he knows he is pardoned. Do you know you are a sinner?"

"Yes," he said, with tears starting into his eyes; "why have I been trying so hard, and making resolutions, and praying, and seeking, except to escape from my sins? My father and mother are nearly broken-hearted about me, but I cannot help myself; temptations can take me away as easily as the wind blows the dust."

"Poor man, now you see what a message the Lord has sent you; it seems to me exactly the one you wanted, though I did not know your case. You must get the SECOND LOOK; there is no rest and no peace for you till you do. Why did Christ die, as far as you are concerned, if He did not die for you? He had no sins of His own to die for. See your sins on Him, and see your pardon through Him, and look at Him, not as a dead but as a living conscious Christ, who is not being put to death, but dying for you and instead of you on the cross. Behold Him looking at you. Nothing can bring out so fully the reality and awfulness of sin as this, or make you feel it; then acknowledge it, and you will feel and know something more—a joy which will lift you out of condemnation into forgiveness and liberty. When Jesus forgives us, we do not cease to feel we are sinners, but we feel forgiveness more; we are sinners still, but sinners saved."

That afternoon my interesting friend found forgiveness and peace, and afterwards he received that strengthening grace which has enabled him to live a happy, consistent, and devoted life for the last eleven years. As a home missionary he has been blessed to many souls.

But I cannot omit to mention one interesting and touching part of our interview that afternoon; no sooner had he found the Saviour than, like a man who has been saved from shipwreck looks round to enquire for his ship-mates, he immediately began to plead for his friend James. He pleaded as if he asked a favour for a friend from a friend, so *really* had he found the true Friend of sinners. He went to James at once, and I know not what passed between them, but in the evening he brought his companion to me with a heart quite prepared to re-ceive Christ, and we had only to point him to Jesus, and encourage him to thank God, and then he realized the truth in his own experience—"This is the gate the righteous enter into: I will praise Thee, for Thou hast heard me." The gate is praise, and by this he entered, who had been a long time standing without and knocking by prayer.

Our friends immediately raised their standard of testi-mony, neither ashamed or afraid to tell of the Lord's mercy, which was as free for others as for them. They went on their way rejoicing and blessing God, and were made a blessing to others.

How many think it presumption to praise God! but God's word teaches us it is far greater presumption to doubt Him and to refuse to praise Him. Men think it humility to speak of the first look which brings us to a sense of our sins; but God teaches us that true humility goes onward to *the second look*. It was after he had been brought up out of the horrible pit that David was able to say: "And He hath put a new song in my mouth, even *praise unto our God:* many shall see it and fear, and shall trust in the Lord." *Psalm* xl. 3.

"Let all those that seek Thee rejoice and be glad in
Thee; let such as love Thy salvation say continually,
The Lord be magnified." *Psalm* xl. 16.

In such and in similar strains he gives thanks to the
God of his salvation. Never can a man see his nothing-
ness so much as when he sees the greatness of God.

THE MOTHER'S PRAYER.

ALVATION belongeth to the Lord, and He can surely save souls by Himself without our co-operation, for He is Almighty, and Sovereign, and irresponsible; but it seems to be His gracious will to work His wonders of grace with instrumentality, which is often very feeble, and sometimes very perverse and crooked! It would appear that He loves to make saved sinners His agents in this great work, that they may be ministers of His saving word to the unsaved, and in themselves witnesses of the power and efficacy of that word; so that the sinner who cannot see or understand the truth may see the saving and happy effect of it in the messenger who brings it. It is to this end also He gives us influence over others, and others influence over us, that we may draw and be drawn to the Lord, and benefit one another.

What influence is there in this world like that which a *mother* may naturally be expected to have over the heart and memory of her child? Even to old age men remember and respect the manner in which a mother's good influence was used in their earliest days. The child is father of the man, and just as a barren and untaught childhood bears its impression throughout life, so on the other hand the good teaching and example of the child's first friend, and her manifest regard for his spiritual as well as temporal good, urged with maternal affection and watchfulness, makes, we may be assured, an *indelible* impression on the soul.

With pious joy and thankfulness to God many a child of God can say, I had a praying mother or a praying father, and their happy memory is embalmed where they would most desire it to be, not in the cold dead marble of the tomb, but in the living, and loving and grateful hearts of their children.

Oh, it is worth while to be a witness for God! and if you have children of your own, to tell them early of Jesus and His love, and to plead for them at the throne of grace, and to let them grow up in the house where prayer is wont to be made in private and in the family, and where their earliest memories were impressed with an habitual observance of the ordinances of the Lord, and they were taught to remember His day, His house, His worship, His continual presence about our path and bed.

As children grow up and mix with others of their own age, too often, it may be, the early blossoms and warm promises of piety which they may have given, seem to fade away, and the tender branch which was trained upwards, pressed by the various burdens which are hung on it, and the strong impulses by which it is swayed, bends and turns aside, and looks as if it had never been trained! But let parents continue in prayer and *persevere in faith!* let them be sure the Lord who taught them to pray for that child, cares more for it than they themselves can care! Evil influences are as changing and unstable as other influences; and they can have but a very unstable hold on a heart which has once tasted and loved better things; and besides all this, the Lord is a prayer-hearing and prayer-answering God, and He can rule and over-rule all things for good, and has promised to do so for those who fear Him, and put their trust in His mercy.

My eye is now on a firm, happy, and consistent Christian, who with his wife, is serving the Lord, and bringing up his children in the fear and nurture and admonition of the Lord.

The thought may now and then cross his mind, as he looks at his children, "Will they burden my heart with anxiety and prayer for their souls' welfare, as I burdened my mother's heart?"

For he had been himself a child of many prayers, and in early youth had given much promise of good; but as he grew in years he grew in wilfulness and impatience, and thought his mother was too religious, too anxious, and too strict, and too unlike other mothers, and so went away with evil companions and among them, and was led to their bad words and worse ways. At times he could not help trembling at himself, and the thought that his mother was praying for him made him uneasy, and at other times he seemed, as it were, utterly unable to check himself, and he was carried away by the stream of temptation.

His mother's remonstrances and tears made him wretched, and he avoided her, and begged she would not pray for him; but she persevered in prayer, and therefore he left her, and took service in a worldly family, rather than remain at home. Oh, the naughty and ungrateful hostility of the human heart!

Among strangers in a new place, he found he had to make his own way, and everything depended on his good behaviour. He could not take license to treat strangers as he did his own loving parent, therefore he was steady and attentive to his work, and he gave satisfaction to his employers by his diligence and painstaking faithfulness to his business. They liked him, and he in turn began to get satisfied with himself, and to forget the good impressions and religious influences which once held him. Being a moral and well-behaved young man, and trustworthy, he was a favourite with his master, and he began to eat, drink, and be merry; but the eye of the Lord was upon him and following him, ever directed on him by his mother's persevering prayer, and so it turned out that our friend was not permitted to get off so easily.

An invalid lady came to stay at the house where he was living, and he was directed to wait on her and attend her when she took the air. She used to talk to him, and ask him about his parents; if they were pious people? he answered "Yes!" Had they taught him to love good things? "Yes!" Did he love good things? "Yes!" and so on.

One day she asked him if he prayed?

"Yes!"

"Some people pray at night," she said, "but in the morning they do not have time; do you pray in the morning?"

"Yes."

All these and such falsehoods, for they were falsehoods, disturbed his mind very much when he was alone.

"What prayers do you say?"

He did not know.

"Do you make them in your heart?"

"Yes."

"I suppose you dislike forms."

"Yes."

"Do you pray to God?"

"Yes."

The lady was very kind, and he was all the more perplexed in his conscience at deceiving her day by day. He began to make all manner of excuses about attending on the lady, and evaded her; but having received positive orders to leave everything else to attend to this charge, he became angry, and gave notice to leave the place. Nothing could induce him to stay, though he had good wages and good prospects, he would go in spite of everything, and so he departed from that situation and soon found another in a nobleman's family. But even here he could not escape the influence of his mother's prayer; for his new master, being a Christian man, took an interest in the spiritual welfare of his servants.

His lordship must needs ask our runaway friend about his soul. He became more and more impatient at this, and finding that he was still pursued with the subject of religion, he determined to leave this place also.

On the morning when he intended to give notice, he received a letter from his mother saying his only brother was converted, and now joined her in daily prayer for him.

This good news did not rejoice his heart very much; and somehow it happened that he did not give notice that day, and on the following day, being Sunday, he went to church and heard a sermon on the text, "One shall be taken and the other left;" what the sermon was he did did not hear, but the text seemed to say to him, "Your brother is saved, and you are lost!" He was overwhelmed with confusion, and felt very guilty and very miserable, and did not know what to do. He remembered how he had despised his mother's prayers, and how he had wilfully refused kindness of Christian friends, and how he had sinned against God and his own conscience. Poor man, his sins had found him out, and he felt himself brought to a stand. He dared not look to God, whom he had so wilfully and knowingly refused. What could he do?

Three days after this, there arrived at the Hall a stranger, an English clergyman; and there was an open-air meeting upon the neighbouring village green, and the people were invited afterwards to another service in an adjoining church. Words of faithfulness and truth were spoken there, and salvation was offered to the sinner on the spot; a felt salvation—to any one who felt himself a lost sinner.

This was a good word for George. Hope seemed to dawn on him now, and after a few more assurances from the word of God, our friend found peace to his troubled soul, and began to rejoice in the Lord.

How little the person knew who was teaching George and pointing him to Jesus, what his past history and experience had been, or how his mother had been praying for him. And perhaps the mother herself was beginning to think how hard it was that God did not answer prayer; a mother's prayer, from a burdened heart for a careless son; but the Lord, who is better than our hearts, and better than our fears, was answering all the time, and even employing one unconscious witness after another to deal with her wayward son. Till by one means and another, all things working together, that lost one was found, and the dead one was brought to life.

Let this be an encouragement to parents to *pray on*, and be assured, as sure as they have a burden on their hearts for their children, and do carry it to the Lord, and are enabled to persevere in this exercise, the very act itself is a token that God is *hearing and answering*, and preparing the ground of the child's heart to receive the truth.

Parents, are you praying for your children? Have particular and not general faith, and may the Lord Himself encourage you to continue to trust in Him and not be afraid; be patient and persevere, and you shall see the salvation of God.

Children, are you the subject of parents' prayers? The Lord pursue you and give you *no rest*, no peace, and no pleasure, till you find true peace and rest in Jesus, and the pleasures that are at His right hand. Would you have your parents put your body into a sinner's grave, while they inconsolably mourn over your soul, which is hopelessly gone to torment? Is this your kindness to your parents, and would you have your own children requite you thus hereafter?

LOOK to Jesus, look and live ;
Mercy at His hands receive ;
He has died upon the tree,
And His words are, " Look to Me."

Come to Jesus, come and live ;
He has endless life to give ;
He from sin will set you free,
For His words are, " Come to Me.".

Trust in Jesus, trust and live ;
Now upon His name believe ;
He has blessing, e'en for thee,
For His words are, " Trust in me."

Rest in Jesus, there repose ;
Shelter find from all thy foes ;
Let His name be all thy plea,
For His words are, " Rest in Me."

THE GOOD OLD GENTLEMAN.

OBSERVED in my congregation one Sunday, a kind, benevolent old bachelor-looking gentleman, in plain old-fashioned clothes, brown scratch wig, and a pair of round horn spectacles; he was very respectable and devout in his manner, and read his book religiously, and attended to the sermon with exemplary quietness and patience.

For several Sundays he came, and coming in good time, was always in the same place, and then he disappeared. I could not find out his name or his lodging, and so he passed from my mind.

Some weeks afterwards, as I was going through a part of my district, in visitation, leaving tracts, I chanced to knock at a door which was readily opened, (it was a house where lodgings were let in the summer season,) I was accosted with a welcome, and told that I had been expected for two days. Not having received any message, I was not aware of this; however, I asked who wished to see me. The woman of the house told me there was a good, kind old gentleman upstairs, who had been very ill for some weeks; he did not think he should ever recover, and he wished me to read and pray with him, and to give him the sacrament.

Being an old-fashioned gentleman, he had old-fashioned ideas about sick-bed and death-bed religion. Some people have some superstitious ideas, and fancy religion is something to die with, rather than to live with; a kind of viaticum to help them in the article of death. Too many such heathen and popish superstitions linger among us.

I went upstairs, and was shown into a spacious bed-room, and there was my old friend, the missing gentleman, with the same brown wig and round spectacles, sitting up in his bed. After the usual complimentary salutations, he bid me sit down by the bed-side, and he began to tell me, which he did at great length, how ill he was, and that he should never get up any more, never get back to his home again. He thought he should die there, "in this hired room," said he, looking round mournfully at the apartment. He had a good estate and a handsome mansion home some sixty or seventy miles away.

"Are you ready to die?" I asked.

"Oh, yes, I suppose I am," he said hesitatingly; "I think I have arranged everything. Perhaps if I could live to return home again, I would alter my will a little; but let that go, what can it matter?"

"Do you think your spiritual matters are arranged as satisfactorily as your temporal?"

"Oh yes, sir, certainly; no doubt about it, oh yes," said he, getting impatient; "oh yes, of course. I never was one of your wild, dashing, spending men. I have always lived carefully and within my income. I have had money to give away to the poor; I am always glad to help the poor, it gives me great pleasure, sir, to do so."

"Yes," I replied, "you look exactly like such a person; your outward appearance quite corresponds with your benevolent words. I quite believe it all."

"Yes," he said, "and I was always brought up to my church, and have never missed the sacrament since I was confirmed many years ago, and I read my chapter every day, and there is my little book of daily prayer," said he, pointing to a little well-worn book.

"But did you never know that you were a lost sinner?"

"Oh, I know what you mean—'miserable sinners,' and 'there is no health in us'—yes, yes, like other people, I am not better than my neighbours; but," continued he in a confidential tone, leaning over the side of the bed, "I should tell you, I have never been an immoral man, or one of the swearing, gaming, smoking, and drinking kind; I have never been exposed to those temptations. Thank God I have been religiously brought up, and have led a steady and regular life."

He was so perfectly unawakened as to his real state before God, and so unsuspiciously dead to any sense of his sinfulness, or his need of a new heart and a new spirit, and so thoroughly satisfied with himself, that I did not know where to touch him, or how to reach him.

I read a portion of Scripture to him from the eleventh chapter of the Gospel of St. Luke, and explained that the Pharisees were so wrapped up in their own traditions and righteousness, that they were not disturbed in their minds, though they did not believe in Jesus Christ. They were not condemned in their consciences, though they could not rejoice like some other people in the miracles of mercy which Jesus Christ wrought in their presence. Then I went on to shew that the Lord accounted for this apathy or *false peace*, and *security*, in a very solemn way. He said, or meant to say, that the Pharisees were kept in that peace by the strong man armed—that is Satan! and that instead of being temples of the living God, they were turned into palaces for the wicked one to dwell and to reign in.

There was only one person who could dislodge that usurper, and that was Jesus Christ the Saviour, who was manifested on purpose to destroy the works of the devil; but they did not believe in Him. Though He was there speaking to them, and though He took such interest in them, they did not know or seem to care about Him.

After a little more conversation on this subject I prayed for God's blessing on the word I had spoken, and besought the Lord, who alone can open the eyes of the blind, and unstop the ears of the deaf, and raise the dead, the *dead in trespasses and sins*, (who do not know that they are lost sinners, who do not know or feel their need of present salvation through the blood of Jesus,) to have mercy on this sufferer, and to reveal Himself to him.

When I rose from my knees, he said he generally preferred written prayers, but mine was not a bad one, and he thanked me in a most undisturbed manner, and bid me call again soon for he had a favour to ask of me. While he was speaking to me in this perplexing manner, my eyes fell on the heading of a tract, one of a packet in my hand: "The Self-righteous Lost, the Sinner Saved." I asked him if he would accept it, and I read the title to him, and went on to read some of the tract too, as I stood by his side.

He seemed to listen and expressed satisfaction and assent at first, but after a time he became silent, and when I had reached the end of the paragraph, he asked me if I would oblige him by reading that again, which I did.

"Humph!" said he, "what kind of theology is that, that makes out that the sinners are better off than the saints? Is that the doctrine you preach, sir?"

I explained, but he did not agree with me, that God changed sinners into saints.

"Oh," he interrupted, "the greatest sinner's the greatest saint—that's what you mean. I don't agree with you, sir; have the kindness, sir, to leave me that tract, I will consider it."

"Christ Jesus came into this world to save sinners," I said; "not to call the righteous, but sinners to repentance."

I went on to tell him plainly that I was in trouble on his account, because he had been trying to prove to me that he was not a sinner at all. I could not therefore give him a kind message from the Lord, as I wished.

"I am sure your righteousness, if it were very much more than it is, would not suffice to take you to heaven."

I begged him to read the tract carefully, and I would ask God to bless it to him. He promised me he would certainly read that tract again.

The same evening I was sent for in great haste, for the old gentleman wished to see me particularly. I must "come at once." I was loth to go merely to renew controversy, but the messenger was urgent, so I went, and found my friend risen up from his bed, and downstairs in the sitting-room, in a very restless state, with the tract in his hand.

"If this tract is right, sir," said he abruptly, "I am a lost man—a deceived man."

I replied, I was sure that the tract was scriptural—"It is better to be judged by the word now than hereafter," and I went over the argument of the tract, and shewed him why the Pharisee was rejected, and why the poor publican went home *justified*, rather than the other. I explained that we must all be born again, that is, pardoned and justified, or never see the kingdom of God; for that which is born of the flesh is only flesh, and all its doings fleshly, and therefore cannot be pleasing, or acceptable to God.

He never heard such doctrine, no one had ever told him this; many good men had dined at his table, they had never breathed a word of this to him.

"Am I a self-righteous Pharisee, did you say, going to—be lost—going to hell? Do you think I shall be lost if I die as I am?"

"Yes," I said, as distinctly and firmly as I could.

He seemed greatly surprised, but the Lord's conviction had already fastened on him, and the circle seemed to become more and more narrow, and very soon he found himself shut up to a dreadful doom; but thank God there was one alternative. He must burn if he did not turn; but he might come to Jesus now as a lost sinner and be saved.

It was a hard struggle for him, but the dear old man was enabled to believe at last, and he found peace and salvation. Astonishment and thanks seemed alternately to carry him out of himself. If he could live to get home to his house, he certainly would speak to his relations, for he was sure they knew nothing about all this. It is a good sign when new converts think immediately of their friends and relations.

He did recover from his illness, and lived to get home, where he did not fail to tell his friends what great things the Lord had done for his soul, and how He had had mercy on him; and his testimony was blessed to the conversion of his brother, and his niece, and it may be to others also, of whom he did not hear.

Before he left us, he was well enough to come to church again once more, where "every thing seemed quite *new*," the hymns, the prayers, the psalms, the scriptures; it was all a new world, and he drew near, *with real faith*, and took the sacrament. He had never come with faith before, and he was much affected by the words: "We do not presume to come to this Thy table trusting in our own righteousness, but in Thy manifold and great mercies."

Reader, do you understand that the self-righteous are lost, and that sinners are saved? It is a strange question to ask, but it is surprising how many in this Christian land need to have it put to them, and explained. They do not understand that sinners are saved, or perhaps they might be induced to come as sinners, and they do not know that they may be saved now, or they would not hope to obtain salvation hereafter! Oh, that the Lord would open the eyes of the blind to see Jesus a present Saviour.

OVER THE RIVER!

OR,

THE STORY OF OLD EDWARD.

HERE are many persons so situated in outward circumstances, that they can look into their future in this world with anticipation, and even joyful hope. To others, the future is all uncertainty; and to others again, a certainty of distress and darkness.

So it is exactly in spiritual matters; some fear to look into the future, it promises nothing, but rather threatens them with soul-stirring forebodings which make them thoroughly miserable. To some, a very large class, the future is *blank*, they seldom look into it, they have no fear, neither have they any hope, and therefore, as the mind ever looks for something definite, they fasten on the present, and engross themselves in worldly business or pleasure, and are perfectly content to remain where they are. They seem as if an earthquake would not awaken them. They really look on more serious and thoughtful people as if they were *nervous*, or too anxious about things, "which ought to be left to Providence!" For they say, "the Almighty can dispose of things."

There are others, thank God, who can regard the future with confidence, and whether they look at this life or the

I

life beyond, a sure hope brightens the scene. They are not afraid to trust in God, who has saved them for a purpose, with a high and holy calling, to an inheritance incorruptible, which fadeth not away. They can say each one, "surely mercy and goodness *shall follow* me;" because mercy and goodness have followed and do follow them. Since the great God changes not, and the Lord Himself is their Shepherd, they shall certainly never want. God will bless them, and make all things, their very sorrows and their troubles, their successes and their mistakes, work together for good, because they fear God, and love Him, and have put their trust in His mercy.

But men are not in this state by nature, nor can they attain to it at all by efforts of their own; *it is the gift of God*, it is the present heritage of His children, and an earnest to them of their future inheritance.

Hear the story of old Edward, who can with rejoicing look over the river, and in the calm evening of his life thoughtfully and with happy anticipation long to be gone —to be where Jesus is, and many of his loved ones too.

One snowy day in spring, there was special service in a certain church in the afternoon, old Edward came to it on foot, a distance of about three miles. He was much interested in the discourse, and was glad to hear that the same minister would speak again in the evening, in the schoolroom. He made up his mind to stay, and offered himself as a guest to a neighbour close by, for rest and refreshment till the time appointed for the service. Much they talked by that fireside of what they had heard in the afternoon; but the old man's thoughts were far away, he was looking into his past history, his many efforts and resolutions, and alas! he saw that the pathway of his life was strewed with broken resolutions and unfulfilled promises. He had just been told how vain are these things to save a man, and the truth was pressing on him.

At length the time of evening service arrived, and he hastened on and took his place where he might distinctly hear. The speaker, this time, having dwelt on the un-

certainty of human efforts, went on to shew for certain
that they would not, and could not save a man.

> "Not the labour of our hands,
>   Can fulfil thy law's demands ;
>   Could our tears for ever flow,
>   Could our zeal no respite know ;
>   All for sin could not atone,
>   God must save—and God alone ! "

These were very familiar words, he had often heard and
sung them; but never had he given much attention to
them. Now they seemed like words of God speaking to
his soul. The speaker proceeded to shew how salvation
may be had, by the *vilest* sinner, not by covering his sins,
but by acknowledging them. For the word assures us
that, " if we confess our sins, God is faithful and just to
forgive us our sins, and to cleanse us from all unrighteousness." " To the Lord our God belong mercies and
forgivenesses, though we have rebelled against Him;
neither have we obeyed the voice of the Lord our God, to
walk in His laws which He set before us." *Daniel* ix.
9, 10.

Many words of comfort and encouragement were spoken,
but old Edward did not know how to appropriate or apply
them to himself.

How often are persons thus impressed in an address,
and for want of some more definite and personal direction
or instruction, they go away unblessed, and soon forget
the words, and lose all traces of those impressions which
they once had.

At the conclusion of the service old Edward went up, in
his kind and reverent manner, and thanking the minister,
said, " God bless you ! "

" Thank you, dear friend ; God bless you too," was the
reply, and supposing that he was a pardoned man, and a
happy Christian, the minister let him go.

How often do people *suppose*, when they might with a
very little inquiry, ascertain, and know the real state of
persons who speak to them.

Full twenty minutes after this, as the last few were leaving the room, the old man was still standing inside the door with his hat in his hand, but his eyes were so intently and anxiously fixed on the minister, that he could not pass him without a word, and he said,

"My dear old man, you are an old pilgrim, you are a long way on, in your journey."

"Yes," he said, "a long, long way on the journey of life; my brothers are gone and most of my neighbours that used to be, and my wife, and all but one of my children; I am past four-score years!"

"Then you are near the river, you are come to the margin!"

"Yes," he said, thoughtfully, "I am."

"Can you see over the river to the other side?" asked the minister; but there was no answer, and the question was repeated.

The poor old man burst into tears, and said, "Oh, sir, I dare not look at it, it is so *dark*."

There was something very touching in the old man's speech and manner.

"So dark, is it? What makes it so dark, do you think?"

"Oh, my sins, my sins: I am an old grey-headed sinner."

He sat down on the bench and gave way to his long pent-up feelings, and wept.

"Well, but my dear friend, don't you know it is a good thing to see our sins, and to feel they are dark, and to mourn over them? It is indeed the next best thing to getting them pardoned."

"Ah," said he, "I have tried hard for a long time, but it's no use, there is no pardon for me."

"I'll tell you what," said the minister, "you do not look far enough; cannot you see beyond your sins? the same eyes with which you see your sins in the way you do, may see the *Blood* which takes away sins. The Blood of Jesus, which cleanseth from all sin. Did you ever hear of the power of the Blood of Jesus? Without shedding of blood there could be no remission, but you know the blood has been shed; you would not have the Saviour die again, would you? Look, that blood is stronger than your sins, just as Christ is stronger than you.'

A long time it took to get the old man to look up unto Jesus; he would keep coming back to his sins and his past life, till at last the light of true life began to dawn on his soul, and his face also began to shine with gladness. One could see the darkness flee away, and the joy of pardon and peace spreading over his countenance.

Presently all was dark again: "It cannot be so easy as that; oh no, my sins have taken deep hold of me, I cannot get away from them."

"Yes, why look at your sins, when you may look off unto Jesus the Saviour? Is there anything too hard for Him? Listen to the words from the book of Isaiah: 'All we like sheep have gone astray.'"

"Yes, yes, that is true, 'and we have turned every one to his own way.'"

"Oh, yes; but now, my dear old friend," said the minister, "listen; here the word of God says, *and the Lord laid on Him, on Jesus, the iniquities of us all*." How is it you believe two sentences of the verse, and not the other? you see you are not believing the word, but your feelings, for when your feelings do not bear you out, you think the word of God is not true! Do you call that your faith?"

Poor man, he cried out, "Oh Lord, help me, help me to *believe*! increase my faith and teach me to *praise Thee*."

The bystanders who had witnessed this moving scene, then all knelt down, and prayer was made by one and another, and soon the old man seemed to take hold of the truth, and he began to praise God.

"I see it now, I see it!" he cried with a joyful heart; "yes, I do believe, I will give praise!" So he went on ejaculating till another train of thoughts entered his mind. "I shall see them again, I shall be happy with them, on the other side of the river. I never felt like this, 'O praise the Lord, O my soul, and all that is within me, praise His holy name.'"

Some of those who witnessed this scene rejoiced with great joy, for they knew from their own experience the change which had taken place in this old man. It is true there are no two conversions exactly alike, yet converted people can recognise one another; whereas, those who know not the change themselves, desire other signs. One among the few there was of this kind, but he did not look the happier for it, or the more content with his supposed better condition. The old man soon took up his hat and staff, and went forth with a light happy step to go home.

"How far have you to go?" asked one.

"Better than three miles!"

"Three miles! it's a long way, do stop here all night;" but the aged man declined, he would rather go home.

"How happy my child will be when she sees me praising God! I'll go home, it is not far; good night, God bless you," and soon he was lost in the darkness of the night.

In the morning it came to the minister's heart to drive round through the village where the old man dwelt, and soon they arrived near a cottage standing in a small garden at the bend of the road.

"There," said the friend who was driving, "that is the old man's house."

They looked at it with interest, for salvation had come to that house. When lo, on the roadside, beside his little gate, stood the old man himself; his countenance beamed with joy, his white head, as white as the snow around him, was uncovered—a beautiful picture to behold.

"God bless you for coming this way," said he; "I came away too hastily last night, I did not thank you half enough for your kindness to me, and so I prayed the good Lord to send you round this way. I knew you would come; bless you, thank you!"

"Thank God, too."

"Oh, yes," said he, "glory be to God."

"Now, can you see over the river?"

"Yes, I can! it's as *bright as heaven* over the river; bright as heaven!" and the dear old man's face shone with heaven's joy and light, as if the brightness which he could see, were shining on him.

Old Edward holds on his way rejoicing—he has his conflicts with the "old enemy," but he can see beyond his sins, he can see the Blood. Soon, if the Lord tarry, he says, he will be called home; and what is more, he is not afraid to go.

Reader, how is it with you? Are you indifferent and heedless about the river of death, or is it dark as hell to you, or as "*bright as heaven?*" Is death the *gate of life,* the porch of heaven, or the solemn entrance to the abodes of the damned? The Lord who conquered death *is at hand.* He is coming quickly, but even before that, He may send for thee—art thou *ready?* Is death as a sunk fence, which you cannot see, but over which you can look to regions beyond, where the weary are at rest, and the wicked cease from troubling?

OH to be over yonder, in that land of wonder,
  Where the angel voices mingle, and the angel harpers ring,
To be free from pain and sorrow, and the anxious dread to-morrow,
  To rest in light and sunshine in the presence of the King.

Oh, when shall I be dwelling where the angel voices, swelling
  In triumphant hallelujahs, make the vaulted heavens ring?
Where the pearly gates are gleaming and the morning star is beaming?
  Oh, when shall I be yonder, in the presence of the King?

Oh, when shall I be yonder? the longing groweth stronger
  To join in all the praises the redeemèd ones do sing;
Within those heavenly places, where the angels veil their faces
  In awe and adoration in the presence of the King.

POOR EVA.

IN a distant and romantic neighbourhood, there is a beautiful spot where the quiet dead are laid beside a crumbling old church, and there are two graves in a particular corner; once there was only one, and a young and beautiful girl used to tend the plants which were growing on it. Regularly and affectionately she came to this grave and plucked away the weeds and dead leaves, and nourished the fragrant flowers which she had planted.

She was just verging on womanhood, and was soon about to remove to the great metropolis, to take her place in the fashionable world, among the rich and great. She had been carefully brought up for this, in all the accomplishments and graces of refined society, and no expense had been spared to make her as remarkable and attractive as possible.

She was as truly amiable in disposition, as she was lovely and engaging in her personal appearance; kind, unaffected, and winning, she was like a bright sunbeam wherever she went—the joy and delight of her parents and friends.

Before she could be "brought out" into the world, it was deemed necessary that she should be confirmed, so that every thing might be done with the greatest propriety and accuracy. Accordingly, she was prepared for the ceremony; and her white dress and the long white veil were not forgotten, and the wreath of delicate flowers for her head. Arrayed in all this she looked very beautiful, and was much admired and praised by all who had the opportunity of beholding her.

"My lovely child," said a relative, "do you know what you are going to do to-day? You are going openly and publicly to renounce the world, with all its pomps and vanities; you are going to be presented to God in a very solemn service, as one who having received forgiveness of all your sins, desires henceforth to serve the Lord alone! Is this what you mean, or is it all an unmeaning form? Will you be confirmed as a child of God, or as a child of the world; confirmed in your sins, or in the forgiveness of your sins; in your worldliness, or in your serious decided resolution to renounce the world?"

"It's only a religious ceremony, aunt," she said; "it does not mean anything so serious as all that;" and smiling, she glided away, and was soon in the carriage with her mother, on her way to the sacred edifice where the rite was to be performed—a rite which might have been the turning point of her life, as it has been that of many others, though they have approached it as little prepared as she was. But, unhappily, she was unwarned and uninstructed, and was permitted to regard it as an unreality and a sham, and religion itself being made subservient, was employed to give all éclat to her entrance upon a career of frivolity, worldliness, emptiness, and vanity.

In due time she was brought out, introduced, and led from one scene of brilliant splendour to another; and her parents' stately house was frequented by much company, so that the poor child's life became a continual round of gaiety. Hours and days and nights passed on with unsatisfying pleasures; nor were Sundays any exception, for foreigners of rank and importance, rejoicing in their "Catholic," though unscriptural liberty, who did not consider the Sabbath as a religious delight, made the house as gay and idle and worldly on the Lord's day as it was on others.

"Will you not go to church with me to-day, Eva?" said her aunt, who had called one Sunday in hope of enticing her to something better; for she was pained, (as well she might be) to see the lovely child thus wholly sacrificed to the god of this world.

"No, thank you," was the reply; "you know, aunt, I cannot go on with all this gaiety and go to church too; it makes me so uncomfortable and disturbs my mind so that I cannot get over it for some time. That confirmation day I could not forget very easily; I was haunted with such serious feelings that I was at first quite afraid to go anywhere!"

Her aunt had no influence over her, though she might have had some. She left that poor child to drift away down the stream of worldliness before her eyes, although the Spirit of God was so evidently striving with her conscience. Her godless parents thought of nothing but her pleasure, and rejoiced in nothing but the admiration she attracted wherever she went; her appearance and manners, her dancing and singing, these were at present all the theme and subject of their thoughts and plans.

The wisest of men said long ago, "If a man live many years, and rejoice in them all, yet let him remember the days of darkness; for they shall be many—all that cometh is vanity." *Eccles.* xi. 8.

Thus poor Eva went on in this career of worldliness and idleness, like a brilliant butterfly, floating on from one flower to another; sipping here and sipping there, pleasures which could not satisfy or make her profitable to any one. It may be said, there was no immorality or impropriety in her conduct, perhaps not; it was more by omission than commission that the poor soul was failing daily before God, and she knew it not.

One day, in the midst of her happiness and unsuspecting glee, she was cantering on her favourite horse, when suddenly a sharp pain made her give an involuntary scream, and as if she had been shot by an arrow, she fell heavily to the ground, writhing with pain; she was taken up and carried to her home with tenderest anxiety and care, and the physician was duly in attendance. He prescribed quiet and rest; but the pain continued so that fever and inflammation ensued, and all was changed in that house.

Music and the voice of song ceased; and, instead of the usual round of pleasure, there was now a hurrying to and fro of another kind, while anxiety and sorrow were depicted on every face. None could say what was the matter, none could soothe the sufferer, or ease her restlessness. All that long night and all the next day they were watching by her side, and the day following poor Eva was easier, and things were beginning to look bright again, when the physician was alarmed, for surely internal mortification had commenced, and that beautiful creature was actually dying. In all her youth, and her beauty, and opening prospects, must she die? He hurried away and brought another physician to consult with him, but his opinion was too correct, and they told their patient that she was very ill—dangerously ill.

"Oh, doctor, don't look so frightened," said she, with an arch smile, "I am indeed better—much better; the pain is quite gone."

It was so; but that indeed was the worst sign in the case, though it was hard to persuade the child how seriously dangerous her case had become; the mother's tears, however, and her convulsive grief were more convincing, and the poor sufferer at last began to believe the fact, but yet she could not realize that she was to die, and that so soon. She was so young, she had not been ill, she did not feel herself to be so bad; but notwithstanding all this, the sentence was out, her doom was fixed, and the reaper was come to gather away this beautiful flower.

Great dismay and confusion now prevailed throughout the house, and the deepest sorrow filled every breast, for Eva was a great favourite. The physician alone seemed calm, and took on himself to advise, as some doctors do not at the beginning but the end of their attendance, that a clergyman should be sent for; as if religion were merely a death-bed ceremony, and the minister of religion one whose occupation it was to teach people how to die, rather than how to live. However, a clergyman duly arrived, who was of the persuasion that she must be absolved by him as her priest, and that she must, for this object, make a full and particular confession of her sins to him. She was told therefore to call all her sins to mind, sins of omission and commission, sins in thought, word, and deed.

She could think of nothing but that she had loved the world too well, and that she had seldom or never said her prayers, and that she had not been to church lately; but all this was too general, she must be more particular. She had not been instructed, poor child, among her attainments to read the Book of God or the book of her own heart; she had not studied these at all, and therefore she knew nothing of her spiritual state. This "priest's" ministrations were more distressing than useful, and his presence as useless as his absolution.

So he was dismissed and another clergyman introduced, who was a friend of the family, and one who had often joined in their worldly company, and partaken of their kindness and hospitality, and, perhaps, rather encouraged than discouraged their manner of life. He soon perceived that his interesting young friend was dying, and immediately suggested that the sacrament should be administered to her; and, accordingly, her parents and relations were assembled to take part in this sacred ordinance.

This minister seemed to have some traditional superstition about the efficacy of the sacrament to a departing soul, and to think it was the proper thing, that these worldly, thoughtless, prayerless, unconverted people should partake of the supper of the Lord, though they had little regard for the Lord of the supper, and had no personal interest in the blood-shedding and death which they commemorated. At this, the most solemn moment of the

poor child's life, just when she was about to appear before
a neglected God, she was thus treated with a sham.   Her
whole life had been unreal, and it was now to end with
such a *heartless* unreality as this.

There was no one there to show her the sinfulness of
poor human nature, and the sin of her frivolous and mis-
spent life; no one to lead her, even then at that late hour,
to the Saviour who died for sinners, and shed His blood
to wash away their sins.   No one was there to point her
to Jesus as the Son of man Who was lifted up, that believing in Him she might not perish, but have everlasting
life; no one to teach her that there is life and pardon
for a look at the crucified One, even as there was deliverance to the wounded Israelite, by looking at the brazen
serpent.   Thus was she left in the darkness in which she
had been brought up, and in which she lived; left without a witness from God, because she had preferred to live
among those who neglected God.

The ceremony was over, and the poor child was now
gradually and perceptibly sinking.

"Oh, mother, don't cry so," she said, "cannot you get
another physician? I am so young to die yet."

All their wealth for the physician who could restore
their darling idol to the hearts of the distracted parents;
but it was all in vain, she was dying.

"Mother," said the poor Eva again, "mother, will you
be good for my sake, and read your Bible when I am
gone?"

Ah, if that mother had read the Bible with her in other
days; ah, if she had brought up that child for something
beyond this world, and its vain pleasures; ah, if she had
herself served the Lord, and trained up her child in
the fear of the Lord, perhaps she might have been spared
to her; or, at any rate, she might not have been eternally
lost as worldlings are, and must be.

This poor mother, like too many others, was perfectly
ignorant of the customs and occupations of another world,
though she was so skilful and successful in matters of this

one. She had no notion of the holiness of God, or the sinfulness of human nature, however polished and refined; or the absolute necessity of the new birth for salvation. She had some loose, general thoughts of the large-heartedness of God, and the manifold meanings of scripture; she had some idea that in a general way all her relations and friends went to heaven when they died,—that dying and going to heaven almost meant the same thing.

Poor Eva's short career of worldly pleasure was soon over; and many a tear was shed for her, and unfeigned sorrow darkened the stream of gaiety, and disturbed it for a little time; but soon it flowed on again, dimpling and smiling, as if no harm were done; no crushed hearts were mourning in retirement, and no neglected soul was awakened at last to feel and know the eternal anguish and misery, of having lived and died without God, without salvation through Jesus, without mercy, and without hope.

Oh, mothers and fathers, whatever your station in life may be, how are you bringing up your children? for this world, or for the next, or for both worlds? for mammon or for God, or for God and mammon? The Lord bless this painful story. It is but one of many such. How many thoughtless souls are engulphed, year by year, even in this land of Bibles and Christian privileges. Within sight of land and within reach of help, souls are permitted to sink and perish; never-dying souls are sacrificed to the demon of worldliness.

MARY:

"THE CHILD OF GOD."

MARY was a stranger to me when she first came to my house, one Sunday afternoon, to attend the service in the adjoining church. Her dress, without being extreme, was after the fashion of the world; her manner, that of one interested and even enthusiastic about the things of God when she spoke on such subjects; but still there was a something which checked free intercourse and communion between us, and we seemed to be fencing, instead of meeting and mingling. I was led to ask her "Are your sins forgiven?" a simple and a very important question, and one full of happy associations to the Christian; but it had the effect of stirring up her prejudice and even disdain.

"Of course," she answered, tossing back her head, and looking rather confused.

"Why is it of course?" said I; "do not be angry with me for asking you, for indeed, it is a happy and blessed thing to be forgiven by God. Was it not a very happy day when He took your sins away? We should never be distressed at being reminded of the goodness and kindness of God to us, in this respect."

"I have been a child of God for eleven years," she replied, looking anything but happy.

"Thank God for that," I said, "and rejoice, for then your sins have been pardoned for eleven years."

There the conversation dropped, for it was time to go to church; but in His own house, it pleased God in His providence, so to order it, that the searching question was continued, for it happened that the subject on which the children were addressed, was that of Joseph forgiving his brethren. We had been going through the history of Joseph, Sunday by Sunday, and that was the point at which we had arrived on that day.

Were the brethren forgiven when they said before Joseph (*Gen.* xlii. 21—23,) we are verily guilty concerning our brother, and knew not that Joseph understood them? They were not pardoned then. Had Joseph forgiven them when they were eating bread with him—when they drank and were merry with him? *Gen.* xliii. 33, 34. No; though they marvelled and looked at one another, they were not yet reconciled, for they did not yet know him, nor had they surrendered themselves to him as guilty ones, troubled on account of their guilt. When they did this (*Gen.* xliv. 14,) and not till then, we find that Joseph could refrain himself no longer, but he made himself known to them, forgave them, embraced them, and wept over them for joy. Not when they were under conviction, nor when they were rejoicing, but when they were come face to face with Joseph, and were all eleven of them fallen before him on the ground, troubled and penitent, then it was that he freely forgave them, and kissed them, and talked with them.

This, as it afterwards appeared, was a good word in season; but Mary went away without making any remark, and I did not expect to see her again. The next day, however, it pleased the Lord that this stranger should be laid on my heart, so that I could not help praying for her; and the distinct supplication which was laid on me, was for mercy for her soul. Other prayers seemed beside the mark; but this one kept my soul engaged before God continually, even through the night and the day following.

Going into the room where I had seen Mary last, on

the Sunday, I saw a strange Bible on the table, and re-
membering that I had observed it in her hand, I took it
up with great interest. Her name, also her address, was in
it, so I sent it to her, with a note, stating the fact that my
soul had been engaged in prayer for her, and that I was
afraid that she was not forgiven yet. I begged her
to come to Jesus for herself, and never to rest till she had
found salvation and peace. She politely acknowledged
the book and the note, and begged for another interview,
which I was glad to give. When I was again in her
company, I asked her for her history, and challenged her
to tell me, if she would, when and how she became a
" child of God."

She readily spoke out, and told me that once she was in
the world, and as fond of dancing and pleasure as others
with whom she associated; that in the midst of her gaiety
she was called to the deathbed of a cousin, who was just
such a lover of pleasure as herself. Her cousin said,

"Oh, Mary, give up the world for my sake; I am lost
because I loved and followed it. Oh, Mary, give it up.
I am lost!"

Soon she died, poor girl, just awakened enough to see
and feel herself helplessly lost—a dying worldling; no
one was near to point her to the Saviour, so she departed
as she had liked to live, without salvation.

Mary wept at the remembrance of that solemn scene,
and said she could never forget it.

"Well," I said, "and what did you do then?"

She answered firmly: "I knelt down, then and there,
by the side of the bed where my poor cousin had just
died, and I called God to witness that I would now give
up the world. I did; and have never had any inclination
to go back into its gaieties and pleasures any more. I
began from that time to pray and to read my Bible, and
to go to church; and I love these things now, better than
I did the things of the world before."

At the time of this change she was led to a church
where evangelical truth was preached, simply and plainly,

and thus became distinctly enlightened as to the way of salvation. She fully assented and consented to what she heard, and therefore became a very earnest disciple, enthusiastic about the sovereignty of God and the doctrines of grace, and all such matters. She understood the spiritual meaning of the Levitical types and offerings; could speak of dispensational truth and prophecy; was very zealous for missions to the heathen, and was also earnestly devoted to many charitable works at home.

There was, however, one little suspicious thing in the midst of all this manifest goodness. She had not much patience with "elementary Gospel sermons;" or much interest in, or sympathy with efforts made to bring in perishing souls; she loved rather to be fed with high doctrines, and the mysteries of grace, with its deeper teachings. There are some men who love to preach exclusively about these things, even before mixed congregations, addressing them as if they were all real Christians.

It is surprising how many people there are just like Mary, who seem to care more for doctrines than for God Himself—more for favourite truths than for souls. A simple elementary Gospel address, with some clear illustrations, was just the very thing which Mary wanted for her own soul's good, more than anything; but, unfortunately, this was the thing against which she was prejudiced; for she abhorred anecdotal sermons.

Well, now I said, "Your story is very interesting, but it is sad, and just what I thought, *there is no Christ in it.* Giving up the world and becoming ever so religious, and being ever so deeply taught in scripture truth, is not the new birth, nor is it the forgiveness of your past sins. Supposing you had never committed a single sin since the day you changed your life from a worldly to a Christian kind, this would not, and could not, atone for your previous sins. You see your sins are not forgiven, and that is why that question seemed to vex you so much last Sunday."

She justified herself, and contended it was not necessary,

to know when her sins were forgiven, and that assurance
is not necessary to salvation.

"But these things are quite beside the simple point;
your story is one of amendment of life, and not of conviction of sin, or surrender to God, or forgiveness. If you
were to die as you are, you would be lost, just as much as
your poor cousin."

Mary rose from her seat with haughty dignity, and
said a great deal which need not be recorded; and con-
cluded by bidding me leave her. I did so, inwardly
praying that the Lord would graciously open her eyes
to see the truth, which I had been enabled to set before
her.

The next day, as I was passing by, she sent for me
again, and acknowledged that she was in great distress of
of mind, and that now she was willing to yield herself;
but, oh! it was so hard for her to put herself in the unpardoned sinner's position. She had passed among
Christians as a living Christian, as a righteous one; not
righteous, of course, on account of her works, for she
knew well enough that salvation was not by works; but
righteous on account of the purity and correctness of her
theology and doctrine. How hard was it for her to take
the sinner's place. How difficult without dissembling to
say, "God, be merciful to me, a sinner."

But however hard it was and impossible with herself, it was not so with God, who sent the convicting
Spirit, by which she knew and felt that she was a *lost
sinner*. Then there was no difficulty, but rather it was a
relief to her, to pour out her burdened heart in supplication for mercy. Her repentance hitherto had not been
"towards God." She had, it is true, renounced the world
and mended her life, but she had never before come to
God as a lost sinner, to plead the merits of the Blood of
Jesus, which had been shed for her.

For nearly three weeks she besought the Lord; till it
pleased Him one morning, when she was on the verge of
despair, to apply the text, *Behold the Lamb of God.* Oh,

how elementary was this; but never before did the word of God give her more joy and comfort. In the intensity of her joy she cried aloud, so that all the household heard her. Mary, the far-advanced saint, was come down to be a new-born child. Now, indeed, a *child of God*. Real living children *are born*, not made, whether by ministerial efficacy, or by self-amendment.

Her relatives and friends heard it, and feared; some were turned to the Lord, and others said that Mary was not to be depended on. But notwithstanding she grew and prospered, and her knowledge of scripture became now a blessing as it had before been a responsibility; and her practice of religion a joy such as she had never known before. She praised the Lord with liberty, as a true child of God, and became a blessing to many souls for ten years, and then departing to another world, left a happy testimony.

Reader, are your sins forgiven? Do not, I pray you, deceive yourself upon such a vital matter as this. Let it be known to you from the Lord Himself, and then you will never be confounded.

OW vast, how full, how free,
  The mercy of our God!
Proclaim the blessed news around,
  And spread it all abroad.

How vast! "Whoever will"
  May drink at mercy's stream,
And know that faith in Jesus brings
  Salvation e'en for him.

How full! It doth remove
  The stain of every sin,
And leaves the soul as white and pure
  As though no sin had been.

How free! It asks no price,
  For God delights to give;
It only says—a simple thing—
  "Believe in Christ, and live."

TRUE OR FALSE PEACE.

———— ✳ ————

ARTH has many a scene of sorrow which we never hear of. We pass along a street, and before a house, and under the very window of a chamber where hearts are breaking, and we know it not; but there is One who knows, who cares, and who has a balm for every wound, and a cordial for every fear. He invites and commands us to cast all our cares and burdens on Him, and bids us not to be troubled, neither to be afraid. Not that we are to have immunity from troubles, nay, rather the reverse of this; but we are to have peace in our troubles, peace such as the world cannot give or take away. "In the world," He said, "ye shall have tribulation; but be of good cheer, I have overcome the world." He puts the good cheer above the tribulation.

One bright spring morning, when the sun was shining, the birds were singing, and all was cheery and exhilarating without, I called at a house and was asked to go up and see a young lady who had been ill a long time. She was the only remaining child of her mother, a widow, who had heard that morning that her daughter's case was beyond the skill of earthly physicians—that she could not recover, and would not survive beyond the coming summer. The poor mother's grief was very touching, and there was another anxiety which began now to press all the more heavily, it was this—she was not sure that her child was saved.

"The only comfort that could remain to me now," she said, "would be that my child might leave a good testimony, a reliable assurance that she is gone to be with Jesus, when it pleases God to remove her."

After speaking such words of comfort and promise as I could to a sorrowing and praying mother, it was agreed that we should ascertain the state of her daughter's mind, before we revealed to her the physician's conclusion. It is better to persuade souls by the word of God, than to entice them with thoughts of heaven, or terrify them to submission by fears of death and hell.

I was led up to a cheerful room, the open window of which commanded a view of the river; and beyond, at some distance, the sand-bar and ocean, with its vessels passing to and fro. The room itself was tastefully furnished, and replete with every comfort; nothing seemed to be wanting there that could give pleasure or ease, and yet with all these, I thought how powerless are earthly things in themselves to give abiding comfort.

There was the young lady lying on a sofa by the window, looking very pale and delicate, though she was cheerful and affable, and declared that she felt very much better that morning. In conversation I found that she was quiet in her mind, and candid and open in all her answers to questions which were put to her; and she took kindly, what was kindly meant. She seemed to be of a contemplative disposition, and had evidently bestowed her attention and thoughts on profitable subjects, and therefore was well informed on the important truths of eternity; but she was not in the least degree *emotional.*

The great truths we had been speaking about seemed to interest her, but did not stir her, and they did not work as living truths in her soul. There was much in which we were agreed, and much kind assent; but yet there was a something which was not satisfactory,— something was wanting, for I felt I had not that spiritual communion with her, which her admissions on the subject of the vital truths of the gospel warranted me in expecting.

There is as it were a kind of free-masonry among those who have *tasted* and *seen* in their own experience, the grace of God which bringeth salvation; they have a spiritual faculty by which they mutually recognize one another, and understand one another. However much they may differ in points of opinion, there is a sympathy and a communion between quickened souls, which is beyond and apart from all mental agreements, and all natural sympathies. Even on most important matters she did not, as far as I could see, seem susceptible of much emotion, but rather was thoughtful and intellectual.

Her convictions of sin were clearly described, but more in the language and manner of reason than experience—more as something she had heard, or read, or thought, than what she had observed and felt. She professed to believe in Christ, but this also was as joyless and as cold as her conviction of sin. I was not satisfied with her, and spoke of our fallen and sinful condition by nature, to which she assented; and of the awful danger of those who are Christless, and she assented to that also. I spoke of God's love to sinners, and His just and holy indignation against sin, and particularly against the damning sin of unbelief, and His readiness and willingness, for Jesus' sake, to pardon the penitent. All this was "quite true," and she quietly agreed to it.

It was a very difficult case, for she was one who had studied her Bible much, and read only religious books; she was of a prayerful spirit, and had ever been attentive to means of grace; so good, and yet to all appearance so lifeless. I could not help shewing her that I was not satisfied; and when I saw that she did not seem to apprehend my meaning, I was obliged to tell her more plainly my suspicions as to her state. She merely smiled; but I was not mistaken about her.

I fear there are too many well-meaning and teachable souls whose religion is no better than this. After reading the Word at the second chapter of the Epistle to the Ephesians, and speaking plainly of the simplicity and

reality of the statements in the beginning of that portion,
I left her to consider the words I had read to her.

The next time I called I asked her, in allusion to my
previous visit, "Has the Lord quickened you? If not,
you are still 'dead in trespasses and sins.'" *Eph.* ii. 1.
Her reply was not satisfactory, so I asked her how long
she had known the Lord? She answered that she did not
know. I asked her how long she had enjoyed peace with
God? She looked surprised, and said "she *always* had
peace," and could not remember when she had not.

"I thought so," I said, gravely, "I was afraid it was
so with you; and what is more, you do not seem to be
aware that this is a wrong kind of peace—a peace before
the war, which is not to be relied upon, for it may be
broken up. That which Jesus gives is a victorious peace—
it comes after the war is over, and the battle has been
fought and won."

She now began to be agitated, misgivings arose in her
mind, and she became alarmed about herself. Her
mother, who had not been satisfied before, now hastened
to the rescue—such is the perverseness of our nature. She
took her daughter's part, talked about excitement, and
said a great deal against people who thought assurance
necessary to salvation, as if I had been pressing that point.
The agitation became general, for "the strong man
armed" who had hitherto been keeping his goods in
peace, began now to be disturbed and to throw up dust.
However, I was thankful to God that indifference and
stagnation were disturbed, for anything is better than
spiritual death; but as I was not disposed for controversy,
I let the matter drop and changed the subject for the
present, till they were calm again. Soon after, with reading and prayer I closed this interview, asking my young
friend kindly, as I left, to pray God to shew *her the work
of the Spirit;* "you know a great deal about the words of
the Spirit, pray to know about His *work.*"

The storm was over now, and she said, looking at me

enquiringly, "You will come again?" as if she feared
that I was angry, and would never visit her more.

"Yes," I answered, "I will come again soon, but mind
you pray as I have told you—will you?" She promised
she would, and with that I took my departure.

On the following day I heard that my young friend
was very unhappy, that her mind was quite upset, all
her peace was gone, and that she wished to see me again,
for she was wretched. I felt for her, and inwardly could
not help thanking God, but was unable to go till the
following day. I found her almost in despair, and her
mother thinking of sending for another clergyman, who I
knew would have made it his business to disperse all her
fears, and to set her mind at ease without the peace of
God. Perhaps he would, moreover, have prejudiced her
mind, as some do, against "sensible convictions of sin,"
and against those who strive to "awaken the conscience."
Such are too often denounced "as making those sad whom
God has not made sad."

However, I arrived in due time, and thanked God for
her conviction; it seemed to be real and genuine. Now
I could with pleasure point her, as a conscience-bur-
dened and unsaved sinner, to Jesus, who alone could give
her true peace. After some conflict with unbelief, and
some delay on the score of want of feeling, she found
peace, and rejoiced with great thankfulness, wondering at
the false religious security in which she had been gliding
on to ruin—as quietly as a lamb. She might have died
also as "quiet as a lamb," perfectly unsuspicious and un-
aware of her danger—soothed to sleep by words of truth,
and her willingness to receive them.

She shrunk with horror at the treacherous danger she
had been in, and the subtlety of the deception under
which she had been enthralled, and was bewildered in
thinking how many persons were being deceived in the
same way. It is bewildering indeed.

Now it was the poor mother's turn to begin an opposition. She rose out of her sorrow and apathy, into animated

zeal against all fanaticism and spiritual excitement, and
declared how her friends had warned her against all this;
also against the danger of insanity, and many other
things. But her daughter was happy and in her right
mind, and that, too, in a very different way to what she
had been; and what is better still, she knew why she was
happy, and could give a good and intelligent reason.

It was evident that she had something *positive* now
instead of the something negative she had had before.
Formerly she was at peace because she was *not alarmed ;*
now she had settled peace because Jesus had paid her
ransom, and she could rejoice in His deliverance. Now
her Bible was become a new book to her, and she was
continually astonished at the new light in which she saw
old and familiar texts, and the way in which they affected
her. The words concerned her now and belonged to her,
whereas before they had only interested her.

Thus she lived on for some time joyfully and peacefully,
magnifying the Lord. The Lord was her Shepherd, and
she did not lack. He led her in green pastures, and by
the waters of comfort; but it must not be supposed that
it was all such pleasant and smooth leading as these
words seem to imply: or that it was all as quiet as it
used to be with her in other days, when she was as still as
the painted ship upon the painted ocean, or rather, as the
painted sheep upon the painted meadow. No, hereafter
we shall have peace from troubles of every kind; but here,
it must be peace in troubles, and in spite of troubles.

Soon after she had found peace with God, it was broken
to her as tenderly as it could be done, that she would not
recover, that the summons was gone forth to bring her
home. At first she seemed to shrink at the thought of
dying, with a natural fear; and wept much at the thought
of her poor bereaved mother's sorrow. This was natural
enough, for religion does not turn us into unfeeling stones,
but rather quickens and deepens the feelings and sympathies of nature; at the same time it gives us grace to
rise above them, and to dwell in " the Rock that is higher

than I." But after a while the bright hope prevailed, and it was well. Peacefully and calmly, like the glowing sunset, though with occasional clouds and rain, her life passed on; and sometimes she talked bravely of her departure, looking with bright hope to the glorious day when she would wake up in the Lord's likeness and be satisfied. Her life was like the river below her window, ebbing out to mingle with the great ocean.

When death really came, the Lord gave her dying grace for the dying hour, and she was calm and triumphantly joyful; she called her mother to her side and asked, in her happiest and sunniest manner,

"Mother, what does that mean, the valley of the shadow of death? There is no valley here, and no shadow, and no darkness; it is all bright and clear, and the light of Heaven shines around me—no more shadow—no more darkness—is this death? I shall dwell in the house of the Lord for ever."

It was a joyous departure, and the poor mother was left with as happy a testimony as she could possibly desire. This is peace!

Reader, have you peace? I do not mean peace with yourself, too many have that; or peace with all men, some have that also; but *peace with God, and the peace of God.* If so, let not your heart be troubled, neither let it be afraid; believe in God, and believe also in Jesus. He will shortly come to you, and for you; but oh! if you have not peace, beware, and think how awful will be the darkening shade around your departing soul, darkening more and more to the outer darkness, where is wailing, and weeping, and gnashing of teeth. Stop, and pray God to shew you the work of the Holy Spirit, that you also may escape and rejoice.

L

THE PILOT'S FLAG.

————⟶⋇⟵————

HAD occasion once to go to a ship, which was anchored in the roads waiting for the turn of the tide, to go up a river which flowed to a great port. Many a ship from different nations was detained in the same place, for the same reason. I entered a small boat, and employed a man to row me out to the ship I named, anchored among the rest.

Proceeding down the river, after a few general remarks, I began to speak to the man about religious matters, and asked him about the state of religion in his village. What did I mean? He seemed particularly obtuse, and my question was quite unintelligible to him, so much so that I could not help thinking, that none are so blind as those who will not see, and none so ignorant as those who will not understand. However, I explained my question, and made the subject as clear to him as I possibly could. If I had enquired how trade was doing, or business prospering, he would have had no difficulty in understanding; but when I asked how the work of the Lord was going on, he did not know.

"Perhaps you do not take any interest in these things, and therefore you do not care to know about them."

"Oh, I know what you mean well enough," he replied, "but I tell you what, sir, we don't allow anything of that kind in our village. We are a set of sea dogs, we don't trouble about singing and praying, and all that hypocrisy.

There was a man here a few weeks ago, he came to sing and preach, and we caught him and took him to the water, and said we would duck him if he did not promise to go, and never return. We are a set of sea dogs, I tell you."

"Do you think," I asked, "that sea dogs are a better kind than Christians, or what?"

His words and manner rather overdid his case. However, I changed my subject, and began to talk for the present of the vessels in the roads, and particularly about a little red and white flag which I observed. Every vessel had the same flag, though besides it, each one had her own distinguishing national ensign. One was English, another American, another Norwegian, or Swede or Russian, but all had the second flag alike.

"What is that?" I enquired.

"Oh, don't you know," he replied, "that is the pilot's flag; when a pilot has charge of the vessel he hoists his flag to signify that he is there."

"Oh, I like that," I said, "it is beautiful. I have given myself up to a Pilot too, and my Pilot's colours are white and red as well; not the water only, but water and blood, the Lily of the Valley and the Rose of Sharon. My beloved is white and ruddy. He pardons with His Blood, and cleanses with the 'clean water.'"

I was very happy and much pleased with the thought, and as I went on to speak, my sea dog stopped pulling, and put his rough cuff to his face to brush away his tears.

"What is the matter with you?"

"You have made me so happy about the Pilot's flag, that I cannot help rejoicing."

"Have not you got a Pilot?" and as he did not speak, I went on to say, "As far as I understand it, when a pilot is aboard, and shows that flag, then the captain is no longer captain; he gives up charge of the vessel altogether, and the pilot becomes captain, and all hands obey him. Is it so?"

"Yes," he said, but no more, and looked unhappy.

"Your ship," I continued, "seems to be called 'The Sea Dog,' and you are the captain yourself, and have no pilot; there is no insurance for you when you are wrecked!"

"Ah," he replied, "I knew better once than I do now," with a very different voice to that in which he had been speaking, "I was much happier then; I should have gone to heaven if I had died then."

"Poor man," I said, sympathising, "come, stop pulling and tell me all about that."

He told me he was well brought up, and used to be regular at day and Sunday school, and had a teacher who cared for his soul, and he was brought to God in early life, and used to sing in the church. He was happy then, and his father and mother were converted people, and his sister who died—"We all loved Jesus, but I was not watchful; then the enemy got in, and I began to neglect good things. I got among idle people and began to love dress and pleasuring, became irregular at the church singing, and was dismissed for that, and so I got on from bad to worse, got abused and scolded, till I went away altogether, and took up with other companions, and went to public houses, and from that to all kinds of sins. I am a wretched man!" and here he stopped.

"Poor man," I said; "did no one come after you with a kind word to stop and restore you?"

I believe there is many a miserable man and woman among the openly wicked ones who know better. They perhaps even outdo their present companions in boldness and wickedness, for they have fallen from a greater height and gone to a lower depth, and strange to say, under all that hardened face and seeming impudent boldness, there is a tender place. They cannot forget the happy days they once knew, and though they put on a cold indifferent face, or toss the head with scorn, or laugh and talk loud as if they did not care, yet there is still a trembling heart beneath, and an aching void within, which nothing can or ever will fill, but that which filled it once, and which it longs for still. I pitied the poor wanderer, and he also was touched with my sympathy and regard for him.

"What a pity you did not show the Pilot's flag, and ask for His orders!" I have no doubt he had had some cries about all this in secret, and now it seemed as if the flood-gates of his long pent tears were opened, and he wept freely.

"That is right," I said, "have a good hearty cry, there is nothing like it to soften the heart, and there is also one thing beside in such cases, and that is to *return to God*, and confess your backsliding and your sins. He is faithful and just to forgive you and cleanse you. You made a mistake in going away from God. When a man who has made profession, sins against light and knowledge, he brings dishonour on God and His cause, and the Lord's people are bound to shew indignation towards the sin, as a public duty. But I think we are allowed to go to an erring brother secretly between him and ourselves alone, to bring him back with humble acknowledgment of his fault, and then to get him restored. Instead of this, people sometimes run a poor sinner down and blacken him, till he runs away from a place where he is known; or he waits till his fault has blown over and is forgotten, and then he goes on as if nothing had happened; but the best way is to make acknowledgment to God and obtain forgiveness, and make restitution or apology when it is possible, and will be accepted.

"I thought," he said, "when I was once converted that I should never be tempted again, and never fall!"

"Yes," I replied, "and many speak as if they expected this from young converts; but where is the scripture promise for it? Generally speaking, people are not tempted before their conversion, they tempt themselves then; but after their conversion, Satan is always watching to tempt them and entangle them, and if they are not armed with the word of God, as Jesus was when He was

tempted, they always fall. But they may arise and come
to their Father, and say, 'Father, I have sinned,' and
become all the wiser against the next temptation.

"When vessels are not steered and handled promptly
and exactly as the pilot commands, they go aground, or
hinder one another; pilot, flag, and all the vessel come to
harm and loss. When you were converted, if you had
taken the word of God for your guide, and if you had
obeyed the great Pilot's voice, you would have been pre-
served safe, and would have remained happy, and perhaps
been an encouragement and blessing to others.

"There is a text in Psalm cxix. which asks this question:
'Wherewithal shall a young man cleanse his way? Even
by taking heed thereto according to Thy word.' People
are apt to think that when they are converted, they can
guide themselves, and that they are to do so. This is a
serious mistake, for it is just then when they should cease
from self-guiding, and may be said to have given themselves
up to be guided ever hereafter, and have been accepted by
the Pilot; they should therefore let Him be Captain, and
watch His beckoning hand, and obey His voice, and never
be afraid to show the Pilot's colours, or ashamed to let it
be known that they are under His guidance. If a vessel
goes ashore with the pilot's flag flying, I suppose the pilot
has all the blame; and how often the blame does fall like
that, instead of on those who made shipwreck by disobey-
ing orders. It seems to me we should be doubly watchful,
for the honour of the Pilot, also for our own welfare and
safety."

The man was silent and seemed to be drinking in words
which he had long been thirsting for; indeed he had almost despaired of ever hearing words of counsel again. I
prayed with him in the boat, and he began to pray too for
forgiveness for the past and grace for the future, and I
believe he obtained answer to his prayer. The Lord
healed his backsliding.

I gave up my errand to the ship for the present, and
went back with him to his village. My new friend and

brother called his wife downstairs, went out and fetched some of his neighbours in, and spoke in touching words of his backsliding, and God's mercy to him.

"And now, God helping me," he said, "up goes the Pilot's flag. I will not be ashamed of Jesus any more, or afraid to own Him."

"Stand up! stand up for Jesus!
Ye soldiers of the cross;
Lift high His royal banner,
It must not suffer loss:
From vict'ry unto vict'ry,
His army shall He lead,
Till every foe is vanquished,
And Christ is Lord indeed.

"Stand up! stand up for Jesus!
Stand in His strength alone,
The arm of flesh will fail you;
Ye dare not trust your own:
Put on the gospel armour,
And, watching unto prayer,
Where duty calls, or danger,
Be never wanting there."

WHY those fears? Behold, 'tis Jesus
    Holds the helm and guides the ship;
Spread the sails, and catch the breezes
  Sent to waft us through the deep—
      To the regions
  Where the mourners cease to weep.

Though the shore we hope to land on
  Only by report is known,
Yet we freely all abandon,
  Led by that report alone;
      And with Jesus
  Through the trackless deep move on.

Led by that, we brave the ocean;
  Led by that, the storm defy,
Calm amidst tumultuous motion,
  Knowing that our Lord is nigh;
      Waves obey Him,
  And the storms before Him fly.

GOING HOME OR LEAVING HOME?

HOW life-giving the sea is to body and mind! There is something in its broad expanse which kindles yearnings about eternity. I was standing one day on a high granite cliff and looking on the Atlantic Ocean. It seemed so boundless and mysterious as it spread off into the far distance, and mingled with the blue sky, so that you could not distinguish where one ended or the other began. While we thus gaze, our souls are transported in thought to eternal things.

"I wish," said my companion, "you would come and see a gentleman who is dying in this neighbourhood. He is a very intelligent good kind of man, and has been a generous employer; he will be a great loss."

"Is he converted?" I asked.

"Well," replied my friend, "that is a hard question, who can tell? people have different ideas about that; some people think one thing, and some another on the subject."

"It is a very important question," I said, "for all that; for you should know that though conversion is not the whole of religion, yet the whole of one's religion and goodness without it, is utterly vain for salvation. No unconverted man is saved."

My friend bid me be very cautious how I spoke to the sick gentleman, *because he was a refined man, and abhorred any vulgar cant,* and so on.

With his permission, I was soon ushered into his presence and seated by his side, in an elegantly furnished chamber over-looking the sea. He was indeed to all appearance an intelligent, refined, and gentlemanly man, but he was looking dreadfully ill and weak. After a few introductory remarks, I said to him in real sympathy, feeling for his state; for there was something about him deeply interesting,

" You are looking very ill."

" Yes, sir," he replied, in a gentle voice, " I am very ill; I thought I should have died last night, I was so ill."

" Were you ready to go ? " I asked; but there was no reply, which made an awkward pause. After a moment or two, to relieve mutual embarrassment, I said, " I was looking on that expanse of ocean just now and thinking about Home, the eternal home of God's children; are you going there ? "

Still there was no response.

" You are in the border land, are you going home ? "

Without raising his eyes he answered sadly, " To the long home."

" I think if I understand you, you mean the grave."

He nodded assent, and looked at me as if he expected me to speak.

" But, dear sir," I said, " that is not a home for the soul; the poor perishing body may rest there in death, but the souls of God's children go home to be with Him. Those who are not His children have their home in this world, and when such die, they leave their home and their possessions also. Going home and leaving home are two very different things."

Again he was silent and sighed heavily. Thinking that perhaps my visit was not welcome, I offered to retire, but he interrupted me.

" No, sir," he said, " do not go away; speak to me."

I asked, " Are you converted ? "

He answered " No."

In case he did not know the meaning of my question,

I asked it in another way, but he shewed me that he understood about the spiritual change which is known by that word, and he believed in the necessity of it.

" Were you not afraid last night when you thought you were dying, since you believe in the necessity of conversion, and knew you were not changed? "

" Yes," he replied, " greatly afraid; but I did not know what to do except to ask God not to take me till I was ready."

" Do you really wish to be ready, as you call it—really in your heart? "

" Yes, I do."

" I am very thankful to hear that, and all the more thankful that God did not take you away last night. I feel so glad you did not die."

" Thank you," he answered, "for your kindness; " and, poor man, he was overcome and began to weep.

" God willeth not the death of a sinner, and because you do not desire to die a sinner's death, He has spared you at your own request. Let us thank Him for this token of His sparing mercy to you; and let me tell you for your encouragement, that the desire you profess to have in your heart to be made ready, together with that light and knowledge which you possess about the necessity of conversion, are equally manifest tokens that the Holy Spirit is striving with you to do you good. The natural man left to himself marvels at conversion, questions how can it be, and thinks it very hard and unkind. Some even go so far as to say, that it is very uncharitable for anyone to insist on its absolute necessity, because it condemns so many good people. But it is evident that Jesus has said to you 'marvel not,' and therefore, in spite of human reasoning and prejudice, you are made willing to believe in it, and even to desire it. I thank God for His kind mercy, and feel quite drawn towards you in interest for your soul. I think I can see that God wishes to save you."

The dear man could not speak, but put out his hand

and pressed and held mine, whilst I went on to shew him
the goodness and kindness of the Lord. I read to him
from St. Luke xiv., of the man—a *certain* man, who made
a great supper, and sent his servants at supper time to
say, "Come, for all things are *now* ready." I then shewed
him that this parable was spoken to one, who made an ex-
clamation about the blessedness of eating bread in the
kingdom of God. We may gather from this that he believed there was to be a great Feast, and evidently wished
to be there, but he had an idea that it was *future*.

"I refer to this parable," I continued, "because it seems
to me just to suit your case. You believe in the blessedness of Salvation and wish to be saved, but you are
still waiting, though you are on the brink of the grave,
waiting for something, as if this Salvation were future. It
is a full, free, and present Salvation, and if you were to
die without it you would die in an unsaved state. The
word of the Lord in this portion distinctly implies, that you
need not waste any more of your precious time in longing
for the future, but embrace the opportunity now given;
it is now supper time, all things are now ready, come:
mark the word, it does not ask you, do you wish to come,
but it bids you, just as you are, to come, and the reason
assigned is, '*because all things are now ready.*' Wishing
and hoping and longing, are not coming. *Come;* turn your
wishes into prayers, take some step to realize your hopes
and longings. You asked God to spare you last night and
He did so; now ask Him for Jesus' sake to save your
soul and to convert you. Flesh and blood cannot inherit
the kingdom, neither can the carnal mind. This corrupti-
ble *must* put on incorruption, and this soul, dead in
trespasses and sins, must be quickened into newness of
life. Only the Almighty and life-giving power of God
can do this for you in body or soul. Ask Him; Jesus
has made every atonement and satisfaction, and now indeed all things are really ready; ask Him, and you also
shall receive."

The sick man seemed intensely interested, and said,

gently, "Am I so near safety as that ? Will Jesus save
me if I ask Him ? "

"Yes, He will, as surely as I am sitting in this chair.
The fact of your asking is practically *believing* in Jesus,
and taking Him at His word. You have up till now
believed in your mind that Jesus had the power, and also
that He had the will, and this you see has *not saved* you
yet; and what is more, never could save you. The leper
in St. Matthew viii., who believed that Jesus had power
to heal, though he had some misgivings whether He would
heal such an one as himself, nevertheless asked Him. He
opened his mind freely, and putting himself before Him
in his own character of leper, he said, 'Lord, if Thou
wilt, Thou canst make me clean.' The Lord immediately
touched him and said, ' *I will*, be thou clean ! ' A living
faith is known by action, a dead faith by wishings and
longings."

At the sick man's request I prayed with him, and
begged the Lord to bless the words which had been
spoken in His name, and then I bid him pray at once to
Jesus for himself, as he had done in the night.

" Do not waste any more time in wishing to be converted,
but ask God to convert you."

He promised he would, and begged me to call again in
the afternoon.

How many there are—"well-meaning persons "—who
are detained, as this gentleman was, for years at this
point. They say their prayers and go to church and do
all kinds of good works, thus pacifying themselves. They
seem satisfied though they have not yet received that
peace of God which passeth all understanding, which
alone can keep their heart and mind. They have not this
peace simply because they hope to get it, instead of going
to Jesus and acknowledging that they have it not, and
asking for it. He has provided it and promised it, why
should they wait for it ? Can God do more than provide
a great salvation for men and send them intelligence about
it, and by His Spirit put the desire for it into their hearts ?

This is indeed going a long way to meet the sinner: what more could He do, that He has not done?

Late in the afternoon I called again, and now without asking any question I could see that the sick man had not believed in vain. He had asked and obtained God's mercy through Jesus, and was full of thankfulness and praise, but he seemed struck with the simplicity of it and kept asking again and again, "How is it I did not see this before?"

This new spiritual life put fresh vigour into his dying frame, and he sent without delay for his relations and friends, and told them what the Lord had done for him, and urged them to seek Him too. He was spared to them for more than two months, during which time, released from that paralysing thing, wishing and hoping, he launched out expressing thankfulness and gratitude to God. Deeply he thanked Him in the presence of others, and recommended Him to their love and devotion. He sacrificed the sacrifices of thanksgiving, and declared His works with rejoicing.

Thus thanking and praising God, he approached the border land of his Home—the Father's House, which is the Home of all His children, to be with Jesus for ever. There was one thing that clouded his joy, and this he spoke of continually. He had *wasted his life;* his health, strength, energy, and influence had not been spent for God; he had lived for himself and his family, and for this world with its gains and pleasures. Oh that he had found the Lord sooner! God had been striving with him a long time, it is true, but he did not know it; and now, when only a wreck of himself remained, in the evening time of his life, God had had mercy on him, and had saved his soul. Now he was going home glorifying God; but his parting testimony to all who knew not God, was: "*Seek Him now, His salvation is full, free, and present.*"

THE KEY OF HEAVEN.

NWRAPPING an old Egyptian mummy one day, some grains of large wheat fell out which had been there for more than three thousand years, and though they had been there all that time they were not dead. They were steeped in water and then sown in the ground, and very soon sprang up and became vigorous plants, which bore large ears of wheat.

So it is that good words of God sown in early years in the heart and memory of children, though they have been buried or carried about for years and years, may spring up at last and bring forth fruit, when those who sowed them have long passed away.

James —— was an old man when my attention was drawn to him, a clever, useful man when he was sober, and one who would and could earn two and three pounds a week at his work, but he was a sad drunkard. His home, which might have been as comfortable as any other, was a miserable desolation, and his wife and children, who might have been above want, and even able to help their neighbours if required, were in a state of destitution and rags.

This wretched old man used to spend his time and money at the public-house without care or regard for his starving family at home, but with all this depravity and selfishness, there was yet one tender place left in his heart,

M

for he loved his youngest child with a great affection. He
used to delight in her and bring her little presents, and
often took her out with him, and treated her altogether in
a very different way to the others. The Lord evidently
in love and mercy to this old sinner's soul, was pleased to
lay His hand on his little idol, and she became very
dangerously ill. Then the poor man was greatly afflicted
and anxious, so he forsook the public-house, and his
wretched smoking and drinking companions, to watch by
the sick one, and saw her languish day by day till she
died. It was a great sorrow, he felt it deeply, and could
not get over the blow.

He was brought to me at this time, looking chastened
and sorrowful, also wasted and worn as drunkards look.
He soon began to open his heart and tell me of his
bereavement, how much he loved that child, and how he
felt as if he never could love anything any more.

"What a mercy it was to take the dear child away from
such a father as you, and from such an influence as
yours."

He did not speak.

"God loved that child," I said, "and saved it from you,
even though you loved it so much, for He saw you would
not bring it up right."

"Ah! never mind," he replied, "it is gone now; it is
gone to heaven."

"Heaven," I said; "do you know and think about
heaven?"

"Oh yes," he answered sadly, "I know there's a
heaven, and that dear child is there; it never sinned."

Without stopping to question the man's theology, I
went on to ask him if he thought he would go to heaven
if he died as he was: "You have a few sins, I suppose;
would you go to heaven if you were to die as you are?"

He answered, looking away from me, "I don't know."

"Come, now, you cannot be so ignorant as all that, I
am sure; none so blind as those who will not see, and
none so ignorant as those who do not want to know: you

mean to say you do not know whether you would go to heaven or not if you were to die as you are now!" As he would not reply, I went on to add, "You know, my friend, there are just only two places for everybody, heaven and hell."

He sighed heavily, but seemed lost in thought. I waited for him to speak, but receiving no reply, I asked him,

"Can you tell me—do you know how your sins may be pardoned? it is an important thing to know how to get forgiveness of sins."

"Ah, yes," he replied, and seemed again to subside into thoughtfulness.

I went on to say, "Some people think forgiveness is to be had through priests, and some by sacraments, some by doing good, and some think it comes of itself when you give up sinning."

"Oh, I know better than all that," he replied, as if he had waked up from a dream; "I am not such a fool as that; no, I was better taught than that. I have a dear old mother in heaven, she taught me how to get forgiveness long ago, in the way that she got it herself."

"Then you have a mother as well as a child in heaven! would not you like to go there too?"

"My mother taught me when she was dying in the bed, how to get forgiveness—" then he paused.

I ventured to ask, "Did you ever get it?"

But he did not heed my words, his thoughts seemed far away, and he went on:

"My mother said, 'James, good bye, my dear, I am going to heaven; will you come too, James? I will give thee the same key that opened the door for me, will you come?'" and then there was another pause.

"What was the key?" I enquired eagerly, but still he heeded me not.

"'I will give thee the key, my son—the key that opened the door for me—it was that simple prayer, 'God be merciful to me a sinner.'"

"Is that the way to get forgiveness, do you think?" I enquired.

"I am sure of it," said he, "my mother was a real Christian, she knew all about that."

"My dear man," said I, "you are quite right; the Lord Jesus taught us that prayer, it is indeed simple and very easy, and within every one's reach; for we are all sinners, and all need mercy; and what is best, the Lord assures us that the man who made that prayer went home justified, that is *converted*, and like every other convert, quite a happy man. It is like telling us the answer to the prayer before we make it. I like your mother's idea of the key of heaven, it opened the door for her, and therefore she knew from her own experience what it could do for you. And so you believe in that prayer, do you?"

"Of course I do," he answered.

"And have you ever used that key?"

Now he began to look confused and ashamed.

"You mean to use it, I suppose, one of these days before you die!"

"Ah, I should be very sorry to die as I am," he replied.

"Then really you have a key to the door of heaven, but you do not care very much to open the door yet; you would rather please yourself and go on living in sin and rebellion against God a little longer. You mean to sin and drink as long and as much as you possibly can, and then when you dare not do any more, you will fetch out your key, and make the best of your way to heaven. You mean to cheat the devil and have God to stand by to help you to do it! You do not care how deep a score you run up against yourself; and you mean to give it all the go by, and perhaps on a dying bed cry for mercy, and go clear off to heaven. This does not look well or right when it is put into words, though it is surprising how many people sin against light and knowledge in the same way without thinking. How many know what to say and what to do, and yet live on in sin, provoking God to cut them down; and none, I imagine, can provoke Him so much as those who have light and knowledge, and sin against it."

I do not remember all I said to that wretched man about the uncertainty of a death-bed repentance; but what grieved and stirred me most was not only the selfish, ungrateful, and cold-hearted way in which he treated his mother's dying love and request, but the cool and daring way in which he despised God and His forbearance and kindness.

"This beats all your drunkenness, and swearing, and wife-beating, all the misery you have brought on your children and their mother; you are a wicked, bad man. And what a thing for you to go to hell with the key of heaven's door in your hand. You will find plenty of company down there, I fear, many who intended to go to heaven, but they had not time to get the key to the door; and some poor things who got the key to the door, but it turned round and round in the lock; it was worn out, it would not open. I have heard people say, Lord, have mercy, who either did not mean it, or said it without faith; they got no answer, and had to die without any mercy. I consider this is the most awful death a sinner can die; it is saying, Lord, Lord, open to us, when the door is shut and the day of visitation is over and past. Mark you, it is not the *knowing* God's will, but *doing* it, which brings a man right. Jesus laid down His life for sinners, and He shed His Blood to take away our sins; this is why God is willing to have mercy on us, not because of our prayers, or our goodness, but *for Jesus' sake;* but we must for our part, fall in with His plan, while the opportunity is still given to us. 'God be merciful,' is in other words, God be propitiated for me, let the propitiation of Jesus be applied to me by the Holy Spirit. The poor self-despising publican who made that prayer knew and felt that he deserved nothing but punishment and rejection, but he pleaded for mercy and not in vain; I advise you to do the same before it is too late."

I prayed with the poor man, who seemed awakened at
last to see his folly and sinfulness, and let him go, telling
him of a meeting which was to be held in the Town Hall
that evening, and I hoped he would make it convenient to
go to it.

At the close of the meeting a man came forward to
shake hands in a most joyful state, and said,

"God bless you, God bless you, I shall see my old
mother and the dear child again; God bless you."

"What," said I, quite surprised, "have you used the
key?"

"Yes, thank God, yes; and it was not worn out, though
I have had it nearly forty years and never used it. God
bless you."

Oh, how good the Lord is to those who call upon Him;
and how wonderfully ready and willing He is to save the
sinner who really and heartily submits himself to Him,
and pleads for mercy for the sake of Jesus.

We should not be surprised at this after all the repeated
assurances God has given us of His willingness to pardon,
after He has told us, that though our sins be as crimson
and scarlet, He can and will wash them as white as snow.
But somehow a little bit of the Pharisee spirit springs up,
and people are apt to think and feel that such a sinner as
this should not be so freely and easily forgiven; that he
ought to have been made to suffer more, and in common
justice, made to feel something of the misery and distress
he brought upon his unoffending wife and children. But
the "free boundless mercy of our God is full of *grace*."
He remembers the sufferings which Christ endured for
and instead of the sinner, and asks not for any more
sacrifice, but rather rejoices to forgive! "Go learn what
that meaneth, I will have mercy and not sacrifice."

Here was a man in whom the good seed of the word
had been laid up, evidently with much prayer and faith
by his dying mother, but like the wheat in the mummy
it could not spring up, because it had not been steeped
and sown by the man himself; when he prayed the prayer

steeped in faith, he was heard and answered, and became a changed and happy man. He mourned for the misery he had caused, and did his best lovingly to make amends for the past. He being changed, his wife and children became different people and his house a different place.

$\mathfrak{B}$EHOLD a Stranger at the door!
  He gently knocks—has knocked before,
Has waited long,—is waiting still;
You use no other friend so ill.

But will He prove a friend indeed?
He will; the very Friend you need.
The Man of Nazareth, 'tis He!
With garments dyed at Calvary.

Oh lovely attitude! He stands
With willing heart and open hands!
Oh matchless kindness! and He shows
This matchless kindness to His foes!

Sovereign of souls, Thou Prince of peace!
Oh may Thy gentle reign increase!
Throw wide the door, each willing mind,
And be Thy empire all mankind.

THE DOCTOR'S STORY.

 WAS called one day, said the doctor, to the house of a friend, a patient; he was an old bachelor, who lived quietly and regularly in his own well-ordered and capacious mansion; his butler was quite a companion to him, for they had lived together a long time as master and man, and had even grown grey together.

On my arrival, I found the old gentleman very unhappy, for his butler was ill, and had been perceptibly failing for several weeks. On being led to his room and presence, I soon perceived that he was sinking, and would most probably succumb; I told him so.

"You are not long for this world; now, are you ready for another?"

"Well, sir, don't you think I shall recover?"

"No," I said, "it is scarcely possible; I hope you have made good provision for eternity."

The old man did not speak. Again I asked him, and he said,

"Master and I have lived together very comfortably, we have never injured anybody; I have been regular at my church on Sunday, and at the Lord's table every month, for many years, and I have done all the good I could, and said my prayers, and all that."

"Ah!" I said, "if you cannot say more than that, I

have no more hope for your soul than I have for your body, poor man; there is no salvation by works, and even if there were, your works have not been very much!"

The man became much agitated.

"What shall I do more?" said he; "can you tell me? I am afraid to die. Can you help me?"

"Yes," I answered, "I will bring you some little books and some tracts to-morrow; my wife has a great many very beautiful little books."

And so I took my leave. I went away, however, with a bad conscience; I could shew that man he was wrong, and must I have books to shew him what is right? This is not the way in which I was treated. I returned to him again directly, for I could not go on, leaving the awakened sinner in his trouble.

"I am come back," I said, "to shew you the way of salvation. When the jailer cried, 'What must I do to be saved?' the apostle had a ready answer. It is the *same for you*—'Believe on the Lord Jesus Christ and thou shalt be saved and thy house.'"

"Oh, sir, I do believe in Jesus Christ; I say my belief every day."

"I dare say you do, but believing in the head does not mean believing in the heart; the jailer believed in his heart, and see what took place. When the sun went down one evening, the jailer was a hardened, careless sinner, who treated his prisoners cruelly; the next morning the sun arose, and the same man was a changed man —how changed! He who had put Paul and Silas in the inner prison, and made their feet fast in the stocks, now brought them out, and washed the stripes which had been so unkindly and unjustly laid on them. He could not shew them kindness enough, he set meat before them, and it is said, 'he believed and his house.' Now, you see, faith produces a change in the heart,—he *was saved!* Are you saved?"

"Oh, no! oh, no!" said the old man, "I am not changed like that."

"When a man is saved," I continued, "his sins are pardoned, and he is happy in the Lord."

"Sins pardoned?" exclaimed the butler, with surprise.

"Yes, of course; don't you say in your creed, that you believe in the forgiveness of sins? Whose sins? Paul's, the jailer's, or whose?"

"Oh, then, I never meant my creed, I never meant my prayers. What shall I do? What shall I do?"

"I will tell you what: just as you give yourself up to me, when you are ill, you do not wait till you are better, but give up as you are, for me to cure you; so give up to the Lord now. He is here. He can save you, pardon you, change you, and make you a *real Christian*. Give up yourself to Him, and ask Him to give you His Holy Spirit, and teach you how to pray and what to pray for."

"But," (interrupting me,) he cried out earnestly, "but I don't know any prayers about that; I only know a few prayers."

"I'll teach you a prayer—"

"Thank you! thank you!" said he.

"A prayer which the Lord Jesus taught us sinners, a very simple one, and one which you can easily remember, and say very truly, 'God be merciful to me, a sinner.'"

The old man closed his eyes and seemed to be saying the words to himself, while I went on encouraging him to repeat it. I said,

"It is a prayer which the *Lord Himself taught*. He really wishes us to be saved; and look, He tells us what is the answer to this prayer."

I then turned to the Gospel of St. Luke, chap xvii., and read the story of the Pharisee and the Publican. He listened as if with new ears, and looked at my face enquiringly:

"Which are you like just now, the Pharisee or the Publican?"

He did not answer.

"You were like the Pharisee when you told me you

went to church and sacrament, and said your prayers and your belief.   Which are you like now?"

The poor man was quite overcome, and covered his face.

"What are you doing? are you praying? shall I go away and not talk to you any more?"

"Oh, no, don't go; I am like that Publican, I am sure. I dare not look up to heaven, I have nothing there.   Will the great God have mercy on me?"

"Ask Him," I answered.   "*Ask Him!* do not be afraid; He has told you to ask Him, and you will surely be accepted and justified too."

"What is that—justified?"

"Accounted righteous before God.   If God forgives you, if God makes you righteous, you could not be better than that.   God laid our sins on Jesus, and offers to lay His righteousness on us."

I knelt and prayed the Lord to bless the words I had spoken, while the man fervently responded, "Amen, Amen."

I then left him, promising to return in the evening, but how changed was the atmosphere of that chamber.   On former visits we talked lightly and freely on indifferent things; but now that we were speaking soul to soul in the presence of God about eternal things, what a solemn influence pervaded the place.   Surely the Lord was there, manifesting His presence.   The savour of this followed me throughout the rest of the day.

I found it easy and a happy work to pray for my old patient, and quite longed for the evening, that I might get back to him again.   I had much encouragement and faith about him.

With such feelings as these I came to the room again, and found him completely broken down with a sense of his sins and of his long mis-spent life.

"I am a lost sinner," he said; "there is no mercy for me!"

"Why not?   Do you think your sins greater than the Lord Jesus? a deeper stain than His blood can wash?

You are looking at yourself, your sins, and your life; instead of looking to Jesus. Why did He die? but for you, instead of you, in your place. He shed His blood and died on purpose to save the lost. Let us thank Him together for His kindness and His grace. If we are unworthy, we should thank Him all the more deeply. 'Glory be to God; Jesus died for me!' say that."

Instead of this, he cried all the more, "God be merciful to me, a sinner."

"But He has had mercy," I said, "He has been propitiated; Jesus has made full atonement."

"Lord, help me to believe!" and soon after, joy filled his soul, and he could rejoice and praise God; and then his first thought was,

"Where is my dear master? Will my master let me see him?"

Master accordingly came and found his man rejoicing.

"Ah," said he, "I am glad to see you so happy. I always thought you were a good and faithful man."

"Oh no, sir! I am a great sinner."

But the master had no ears to hear, or eyes to see, or heart to care for these things; he was quite satisfied with his own harmlessness and goodness.

In a few weeks the old butler departed, rejoicing in God, a sinner saved by grace. His body was laid with all respect and reverence in the grave, and his master felt lonely and desolate.

"One of these days I must go too, and people will come back from my funeral," said he, and he threw himself back in his old accustomed chair. "Shall I ever see old Frank again?"

I did not like to interrupt my friend's grief, but at last I ventured to say, "He is happy now; you would not have him back?"

"No, no!" he said, "that would be selfish. I must try and be as good as he was."

"Do you think you shall save yourself by that means?"

"Yes, certainly; why not?"

"People are not saved by trying to be good, but by coming to God as lost sinners, that they may be saved by Him, and made good by Him."

However, he could not or would not see. "Certainly a man must do his best, certainly he would try."

He went on in his own quiet way, with family prayers and weekly public service, till a few months after; when I was sent for to his house again in great haste; but it was all too late, my friend was gone, without a struggle or a groan, without any fear for his unpardoned sins, without a change of heart, without any alarm at going out of a state of probation! He was gone. He never knew he was a sinner, while he might have received pardon for his sins.

Such was the doctor's story, which I have given in my own words and manner, though the facts and circumstances are his. The poor master never knew he was a sinner! No doubt, like many others, had you spoken to him on the subject, he would have told you how weak and sinful he was, though in all probability he would not have liked any one else to say the same of him. If he had only known and understood that he was a lost sinner, and altogether unable to save himself, he would have sought for the Saviour to save him. It is a faithful saying, and worthy of all acceptation, that Christ Jesus came into the world (and He is here still) to save sinners.

THE DYING GIPSY.

HE great and good Countess of Huntingdon said the letter M saved her. She thanked God that the Bible did not say "not any," but "not *many* noble" are called. Indeed it is so, "Not many wise men after the flesh, not many mighty, not many noble, are called; but God hath chosen the foolish things of the world to confound the wise; and God hath chosen the weak things of the world to confound the things which are mighty, and base things of the world, and things which are despised hath God chosen, yea, and things which are not, to bring to nought things·that are; that no flesh should glory in His presence."

But it should be well understood that the words, "Not many noble are called," is not intended to be the announcement of a doom or fate, but the declaration of a fact; for unhappily it is too true that the noble, and the wise, and the gifted are too apt to lean on their own resources and gifts, instead of trusting in the Giver of gifts; that is, God, who is after all the only Fountain of all blessings, whether they come to us by visible and known instrumentality or otherwise.

It is surprising how accessible the unseen Lord is, and how present, to all who call on Him, rich poor, noble or simple. He is no respecter of persons, but in every position, *whosoever* calls on the Name of the Lord is delivered, and what is more, has the joy of knowing it.

N

Some came to Jesus when He was on earth, saying, "If Thou wilt;" and some came doubting His power, saying, "If Thou canst do any thing;" but He never sent any one empty away, however ignorant, who came to Him with expectation of deliverance. He is the same still as He was then, if we come to Him just as we are, with all our sins and ignorance, our entanglements and wicked-nesses, we also shall find Him a present Saviour, more willing to give than we are to ask, more willing to save than we are to be saved.

I was called one day to see a poor gipsy woman, who was dying in a state of great destitution and distress. She could not be received in the hospital, because hers was a hopeless case, and she was near her end. She gave a pretty clear account of herself, her illness and her manner of life; but in respect of her soul and her spiritual con-dition, she was in thick darkness and ignorance.

"You know, my poor woman," I said, "that you are dying, but do you know it is only your poor suffering *body* which will die and become insensible? your soul can-not die in that way; it must live somewhere, and live as long as God lives. Where is it to live?"

She did not know, but she seemed to have some vague idea that because she had been baptized, there was some kind of a hope for her soul. She thought she would have a "decent Christian burial," and that her body would rise again; but when she had put her vague inconclusive ideas into words, she easily saw how unsatisfactory and insufficient they were.

"I suppose," I said, "you have committed some sins since you were baptized; what about them, and how are they to be forgiven? There is no repentance in the grave, and no forgiveness there. If your never-dying soul leaves your body before you are saved, you cannot be saved after you die; you will be lost for ever. It is a dreadful thing to die like this. I will tell you what becomes of everyone who dies unsaved; it is this: his poor body is put into a sinner's grave, and his soul sent away to a place of torment, where there is wailing, and weeping, and gnashing of teeth, and despair. By and bye, from this miserable place, the soul will be summoned by the archangel's trump, which will also raise up the body from the grave, though it may have gone to dust ages before. Then soul and body raised and joined together again, will stand before the great white throne, to hear the sentence, 'Depart, ye cursed, into everlasting fire, prepared for the devil and his angels.' What a dreadful prospect this is. I do not think it is kind to hide these things from you, when God in His kindness has plainly declared them, and forewarned us all."

"Oh, what shall I do," said the poor woman, interrupting me, "what shall I do to be saved?"

She gave me to understand that she had heard enough at different times in her life to know and feel that what I had said was all true.

"What shall I do," she cried; "if I die to-night, must I be lost like that for ever?"

"No, my dear woman," I said, "you need not, for Jesus Christ came into this world and died upon the cross, to save such sinners as you and me. He shed His precious blood to wash our sins away; all our sins, long before they were committed, were laid on Him, and He bore them and the punishment for them, instead of us. He died that we might live."

I then set Jesus Christ and Him crucified before her, as the Lamb of God which taketh away the sin of the world, and endeavoured to shew her, her own personal interest in Him. She was deeply interested, and acknowledged that she had heard most of these things before, but she had never arranged them in order in her mind, and never applied them to herself and her present need.

By this time she was getting exhausted, so I prayed earnestly, begging the Lord to help this poor sufferer, and reveal Himself to her in all His pardoning love and mercy, and then I rose to take leave of her for a few hours, promising to call very early in the morning to see how she was.

"Think of what I have said to you, and ask Jesus to save you; He is here."

So saying, I took up my hat to leave, when I heard her say something in a very faint voice.

"What did you say?" I enquired.

"Pray the Lord God," she answered, "not to take me away to-night."

"Why not?" I asked; "what will you do if you are spared to-night?"

"I will ask Him to save my soul for Jesus' sake."

Immediately I knelt down and made the request she had asked, and then departed.

The next morning on my return, I found her in the deepest distress about her soul; but her husband, whom I had not observed crouched in the corner of the unfurnished room the night before, was there too, rejoicing in the forgiveness of his sins. He had witnessed all that had passed the evening before, and had heard what I had said to his wife, and during the night he had joined her in prayer for salvation, and with simple child-like faith, by the grace of God, he had found salvation. He was rejoicing in the morning, and she, poor woman, all the more miserable because she had not found it yet. She was now thoroughly awakened to a sense of her soul's danger and misery, and so different to what she had been the night before, that I could not help praising God for the work of the Holy Spirit begun in her soul.

I said to her, "Angels rejoice over sinners repenting, and they are rejoicing over you at this moment. Let us thank God together for His mercy to you. He wounds the soul only to heal it, and kills to make it alive. He makes us feel our sins and danger, that He may pardon and deliver us."

With words of cheer and comfort I encouraged her to *believe* in Jesus for herself.

"He died for you, thank Him yourself. He loves you

and wishes to save you; thank Him as well as you can."

She soon began to praise God for the salvation of her soul, and weak as she was in body, it was surprising to see what new energy was given to her. She sent her husband out to call some others of the gipsy band who were lodging in the neighbourhood, and "the boy who had seen the bright angel in his dream." Some of them came immediately, expecting to witness her death, but instead of this, they were astonished to hear her pour forth wonderful words of thanksgiving and praise to God for saving her soul; and in a simple and most earnest way, she then and there began to tell them what the Lord had done for her soul, and entreated them, though they were dark and ignorant, as she had been, to do as she had done, and she was sure they would find the same salvation.

Day after day she bore her joyful testimony, and nine persons, one after another, were converted to God through her instrumentality at her bed-side; and while her life was prolonged, it was very edifying to see how wonderfully she was taught of God, and how distinctly the once ignorant gipsy woman bore testimony to the Truth as it is in Jesus. People were continually in that room, praying and blessing God with her. It was indeed a wonderful and joyful thing to behold these people, poor and ignorant as they were, so filled with the love and praise of God.

Some weeks afterwards, on a Good Friday afternoon, a funeral procession passed down the street towards the cemetery. It was hers, and great interest was awakened on her account, so that many looked out to see, and a very touching sight it was to behold the husband, and nineteen others following the poor workhouse coffin, crying and rejoicing as they went along. They stopped and sang a short hymn before they left the street, and then again when the funeral service was over, they sang at the grave, and left the dust to return to its dust, while the released and happy spirit was rejoicing above.

This was the beginning of an interesting work of God among the gipsies in that place, and who can tell where it will stop? It is a simple narrative, and shews how ready and willing is God to hear prayer, and own and bless His word, when it is received in simple child-like faith, when there is no reasoning to hinder truth, or prejudice to harden the heart, prejudice with which the god of this world is ever seeking to blind the minds of those who will not believe the word of God delivered to them.

The poor woman believed, and was saved. She came with simple faith, and had personal and direct intercourse with Jesus as her Saviour; between Him and her soul there was nothing to intercept the blessing, no church, or sacrament, or priest, for these are not intended for salvation, and would therefore have hindered her as they do others. The sinner's salvation or the soul's justification is by faith only.

Romanism and all churchism is willing to go as far as to say we are *justified by faith,* but there they stop, omitting the important "only," which is in itself an impassable gulf; if it is added, the church system fails; if it is excluded, the soul must fall. The doctrine of justification by faith only, is the counterpart of the atonement; they must stand or fall together; deny the former, and then the death of Christ remains as one cause among others, of salvation, but not *the sole cause;* deny the latter, and then the crucified One may be to you a hero, or philanthropist, or an example, but not a Saviour, and the only Saviour Jesus.

How many who seek are not able to find salvation. It is because they do not just simply receive the word as from the Lord and act upon it. This poor woman believed the simple story of the Cross, and with appropriating faith applied it to herself, and soon burst out into thanksgivings. The Spirit sealed her faith, and confirmed her praise, and she knew and felt she was saved.

Reader, if you do not know this in your experience, do not waste time and opportunity in cavilling and disputing, but do as this woman did, and you also shall know what she knew, to the joy and deliverance of your soul. Indeed it is not by works of righteousness which we do, or can do, nor by joining churches, or by obeying ordinances, but simply by believing on the Lord Jesus Christ for yourself. The dying Israelite only looked at the brazen serpent and he was healed. Virtue came from the brazen figure and made him whole; so virtue can come from the crucified One, by the operation of the Holy Ghost, to save every believing sinner.

> "Then take with rejoicing from Jesus at once,
>   The life everlasting He gives,
> And know with assurance thou never canst die,
>   While Jesus thy righteousness lives."

JARROLD AND SONS, PRINTERS, NORWICH.

THERE is life for a look at the Crucified One,
  There is life at this moment for thee;
Then look, sinner, look unto Him and be saved,
  Unto Him who was nailed to the tree.

      Look! look! look and live!
      There is life for a look at the Crucified One,
      There is life at this moment for thee.

It is not thy tears of repentance or prayers,
  But the *Blood*, that atones for the soul;
On Him, then, who shed it, thou mayest at once
  Thy weight of iniquities roll.

Then doubt not thy welcome, since God has declared
  There remaineth no more to be done;
That once in the end of the world He appeared,
  And completed the work He begun.

But take, with rejoicing, from Jesus at once,
  The life everlasting He gives;
And know with assurance thou never canst die,
  Since Jesus, thy righteousness, lives.

Printed in December 2022
by Rotomail Italia S.p.A., Vignate (MI) - Italy